By Design

By Design
How the Bible Fits Together

JAY WATSON

ISBN: 978-1985792227

Know. Grow. Do.

Contents

Acknowledgments

In 2013, I had an idea for a sermon series; this book is the end result. Rob Buntain was my associate pastor when the concept first occurred and he was a valuable source of input and encouragement. Rob, thank you for your friendship and help.

There are many people who have helped finish this book. Mark Jenkins, Blake Neill, Justin Phillips, and Jon Dockery have all been immensely valuable. Thank you for letting me call in this favor. A man's worth is greatly increased by his friends. I'm rich! Megan Phillips, thank you for making this book look beautiful and smart. Brenda Noel of ECHO Creative Media, thank you for completing the finishing touches.

To Life Community Church, I am humbled and honored to be your pastor. This book was inspired by you. I long for us to know

God together, grow in faithfulness to Him, and do things that bring Him glory. Thank you for letting me do this alongside you.

The truth is, this book would never have been a reality without Kevin Johnson. You have been a sounding board, editor, and protector of good. You've handled all my insecurities with grace. I hope we get to collaborate and create for the glory of God many more times. Thank you for pushing me to be better.

Shantel, you are God's greatest gift to me. I love you with all of my heart. I'm so relieved the girls look like you. Thank you, Hannah Chayse and Hope, for being my biggest fans. You three are my highest calling.

Designed For You

This book is for you. It's for the person who has gone to church their entire life and never quite figured out how it all fits together. This book is for the mom who is embarrassed that her children know more Bible stories than she does. This book is for the man who has never really opened the Bible but wants to know more about God. This book is for people with doubts. While they certainly don't have answers for everything, I believe these chapters can help everyone.

God designed a plan even before creation to save the world. From the beginning to the end, the Bible fits together. It is not a collection of advice meant to make our lives better. It isn't an accidental collection of some of the best stories ever told. The Bible is intentional. It is truth from God for us, by design.

This book is meant to be read next to the Bible. Grab your Bible, get something to write with, and take your time. The chapters aren't long, and this book is written with simplicity and clarity. Write your questions and thoughts all over the margins.

Finally, everything in the Bible is about Jesus. This book is too. I hope it brings you closer to Him.

One Bad Apple

Reading Genesis is often an uphill battle. I have so many questions. Other parts of the Bible appear to have more practical life application—things I can use to understand how God wants me to live. I sometimes think the problem with Genesis and the Old Testament is that there isn't enough useful information for my faith. But in reality, the problem is not Genesis; the problem is me.

If we try, we can learn much about God in Genesis. The creation story reveals the God who made everything. And the account of Adam and Eve slipping up and ruining the perfect world reveals God's nature. In between moments of miraculous creation, we see the heart of God revealed in His love for His children.

Nothing is an accident. Everything is by design.

"In the beginning, God created the heavens and the earth" (Genesis 1:1).

God created everything. When I stop to consider this, it feels impossible to grasp. Sometimes the beauty of creation sneaks up on me. I'm surprised when I'm driving down the road and discover a scene that appears crafted by an artist. Watching leaves float on the wind in autumn is mesmerizing. When I find rock formations that seem like they are carved by hand, I can't help but be impressed by God's power. His design is overwhelming. It is completely different than anything else. I have a hard time fully appreciating the detail, precision, and beauty.

I feel insignificant when I consider the beauty and detail of creation. The ocean seems to never end. The stars in the sky tower over Earth. Standing at the base of a mountain is intimidating. Even the small things make me feel tiny in comparison to what God has done. I could never count every blade of grass in my front yard. Pebbles, salt, and sand seem immeasurable. Creation required something vastly beyond our ability. Creation is something different. When I realize who created everything, this makes sense. Before the beginning, before the heavens and earth existed, before the universe whirled into motion, God was. How does this make you feel?

What we know about God comes from what He reveals to us. And God reveals details about Himself in creation. His creation is His story by His design. And His artistic endeavor isn't just about beauty; God also designed it to function. Every moment of creation is dripping with purpose. Think about how all life works together to maintain existence. Every minuscule insect has a purpose and is designed to work in harmony with the rest of the world. Animals are no different. They all work together to keep a balance in all life. Animals provide humans with food, raw materials, and even assistance for life tasks. The ability of vegetation to convert the gases that make our atmosphere connects every living thing. God has filled His creation with intentionality.

God is different. The "otherness" of God is amazing. God created all things by simply speaking them into existence. Everything that was, is, and will be is from God.

Not only did God create everything on Earth, but in His infinite power, He also created the heavens above: the moon, stars, galaxies, and the overwhelming immensity that is the universe. He spoke and it happened. More than mind-blowing, it is impossible to fully appreciate and understand.

Read Genesis 1:26—2:1.

Genesis 1:26 introduces a peculiar phrase: God created man *in His own image.* Scripture teaches that God only made humans in this way. Human beings are made in the likeness of God. God then gave humans the task of ruling over the earth and overseeing the creatures in it. God called human beings to occupy the land, to multiply, and to take dominion over all things. Part of God's design involves the human desire for sex. We are to create more life and bring more dominion over all the earth. God made this world for us, for our enjoyment. It meets our physical needs while wowing us with God's creativity.

"And God saw everything that he had made, and behold, it was very good. And there was evening and there was morning, the sixth day"
(Genesis 1:31).

We often step past this important truth: In the beginning, all of creation was "very good." There were no accidents. There was neither pain nor strife. At this moment, it's all good. Man, creatures, and God all lived in relationship and in harmony.

"And the Lord God commanded the man, saying, 'You may surely eat of every tree of the garden, but of the tree of the knowledge of good and evil you shall not eat, for in the day that you eat of it you shall surely die'"
(Genesis 2:16, 17).

At some point as you read the creation story, it is natural to ask, "Why?" Why does God do things the way He does? Why does God make Eve from a rib? Why does God make a tree that will kill people?

Up to this point, Adam and Eve are without sin and scheduled to live forever. They are made in the image of God. But there is one tree with fruit they are not supposed to eat. If they do, they will die.

Had there not been a tree like this, Adam and Eve would not have had free will—following God would not have been optional. But God did not make mindless machines devoid of free will. God made humans in His image. He created man and woman to have a relationship with Him. Obedience was a choice. And Adam and Eve chose disobedience.

Read Genesis 3:1–19.

This was a willful act of disobedience. The serpent tempted Adam and Eve, but he didn't force them do anything. They acted on their own desires. They ate the fruit.

It's interesting to consider what the specific sin was. It wasn't just fruit-eating. It's not as if all of this could have been avoided by a different diet. The sin was really something familiar to all of us. Eve and Adam made a choice to put themselves in God's place. They wanted to know everything. They desired to become their own authority, to become God and to take His glory for themselves. They wanted the position, the knowledge, and the power.

It only took three chapters for humanity to mess everything up. Genesis began with God speaking life into existence, and, almost immediately, humans tried to become like God. Their coup attempt began by eating the fruit from the tree of the knowledge of good and evil. It sounds ridiculous: trying to become like God by eating fruit.

But Adam and Eve didn't gain power. Instead, they lost their innocence and found shame. They felt guilty, exposed, and vulnerable for what they had done. The results of disobeying God were painful to discover. Eve and all who would follow now experience difficulty and pain in bearing children. Everyone is born with sin. Man experiences great difficulty in his work. To this day, we struggle with wanting to subdue life only to feel beaten down and unsuccessful. Pain and difficulty occur in the God-ordained means of provision and protection and in moments that should be full of joy and satisfaction. And the ultimate result of choosing to go against God is death.

Pushing the fast-forward button a few thousand years makes the effects of sin painfully evident. We live in a world that is far less than it is supposed to be. It has fallen from perfection. Adam and Eve's choice cursed and corrupted our earth. We are born into this world selfish; it is part of who we are. We constantly struggle to replace God on His throne. We are forced to subdue the land because the land has revolted; the thistles and thorns have grown strong over the perfect fields God designed. Earth is no longer perfect. It is ravaged with disease, sickness, and natural disasters. It is broken and each day we experience the painful effects. Decay has set in. Each moment brings new and creative ways for us to sin boldly. The forms of death we face are both unnatural and unintended.

The creation story fills us with amazement and wonder; however, the story of Adam and Eve fills us with doubts and despair. Their story is of the loss of what should have been. From the time of Adam and Eve, all seemed lost, especially hope.

But God had a plan for His people. God promised hope. Even while the world received punishment through the choice of Adam and Eve, the Creator of the universe showed compassion and extravagant love for us.

"The Lord God said to the serpent, 'Because you have done this, cursed are you above all livestock and above all beasts of the field; on your belly you shall go, and dust you shall eat all the days of your life. I will put enmity between you and the woman, and between your offspring and her offspring; he shall bruise your head, and you shall bruise his heel'" (Genesis 3:14, 15).

This moment shows God as someone we can trust. It is a foreshadowing of the entire story of the Bible after the fall. There is hope. God speaks of a baby coming from a womb who will grow up and crush the head of the serpent. It is not coincidental that Paul later writes that "the God of peace will soon crush Satan" (Romans 16:20).This passage from Genesis 3 tells us that the serpent will continually attack the offspring of the woman. There will be pain and suffering. But ultimately, the offspring of Eve will crush and destroy the serpent. God revealed as far back as Genesis that He had a plan. This plan weaves throughout all of Scripture and is much bigger than it appears. It even started before Genesis 3. It began when God made man:

"Then God said, 'Let us make man in our image, after our likeness'" (Genesis 1:26).

Two words in this sentence are revealing: "us" and "our." This is one of the first places in Scripture where we get a taste of the concept of God as Trinity: three persons, one God. The Father, the Son, and the Holy Spirit are present. Genesis 1:26 is another clear example that God is completely different in His very being from anything else.

Jesus is present in Genesis 3. He was there! God, in His infinite wisdom and love, offered hope in the darkest moment of history.

———

This story can be bittersweet. It is fascinating to consider life on an earth that was "very good." In the Bible, God creates something and calls it "good." After making everything, before the fall of man, God says His creation is "very good."

What if there was no pain or struggle in the simplest things? A place with no sinus pressure or asthma sounds terrific. Imagine having a relationship with another person that doesn't involve selfish motives. What if you never had to pull a weed in your front lawn? Think about never understanding or experiencing death. A world without harshness, suffering, and imperfection sounds "very good."

When we think about what could have been, it is heartbreaking to know we chose selfishness and power rather than God. The story of the fall of mankind is terrible, but not without hope. The first thing God revealed as He was handing out punishment was the hope we have in Jesus.

I've always imagined a sad Creator having to deal with His disappointing children. When I do something wrong and get caught, my first instinct is to think about the consequences. But God's first words are filled with hope. There will be suffering, yes; but one day, God will destroy the serpent—He will crush his head. This story gives hope for the world to come. It reveals something vital about the nature of God: He loves us first. Even in the midst of our sin and rebellion, God cares for us.

It is easy to think that if I follow the rules and show kindness to others, God will like me. We think God's love is dependent on our good choices. When I do wrong, I feel just like Adam and Eve: guilt and shame fill my mind and I try to figure out how I can cover up and hide what I've done. I feel exposed and vulnerable.

I may not be filling my stomach with the wrong kind of fruit, but I have no trouble filling my days with more of me. My selfish thoughts carry me to selfish plans. Step after step, I climb upon my own throne. In the quiet moments of understanding, I don't usually think about God's love. I think about God's punishment, which I deserve. But God starts with love. He starts with hope. God has revealed that He loves us, even when we don't love Him.

God cares about you even when you are doing wrong. God loves you even when you only love yourself. God never stops loving you. God's love is present in creation and the fall. Even after Adam and Eve rebelled against Him, God gave them hope.

I don't know that I've ever spent time reading Genesis looking for love, but there it is. God loves you. God loves you because He made you; He loves you no matter what you've done. God's love isn't given as a condition of your behavior; instead, it is unconditional because of who He is. His design is love.

Jesus is in Genesis. We will also find Him everywhere else in Scripture. His story weaves throughout time and history to reveal an intimate picture of love. Through God's design, hope springs forth from certain death.

Reflection

Read Genesis chapters 1–3 again. Take your time. Think about what's been connected so far in God's story of redemption. Slow down; pretend this is the first time you've read this. Think about the words you are reading.

1. Consider the intentionality of God's creation plan. Why do you think God created the world in this specific progression?
2. How does the Serpent's temptation highlight humanity's selfish nature?
3. What specific ways in chapter 3 do you see God protecting Eve and Adam despite their sinfulness?
4. When you look back on your life, how has God been intentional in showing you His love?
5. How does God's consistent love encourage you today?
6. How does the revelation that God loves you even in the middle of your sinful actions change the way you think and feel about God?

The Ark and the Tower

Everyone knows about Noah and his ark. We decorate our children's rooms with giraffes with intertwined necks and monkeys holding hands as they walk into the side of a boat. A giant rainbow canopies the whole scene. It looks like the happiest place on earth; but the real scene was quite different.

Think for a moment about what actually happened. I wonder how many people crowded around the boat as it first started to float. I imagine bloated dead bodies bumping up against the side of the hull by day eleven. I bet it did not smell pleasant on that boat! I cannot fathom what it would be like to mourn the loss of the entire population.

The mural on the wall in the preschool classroom contains none of these unpleasant realities. The story of Noah is famous; but we have sanitized it. We discover something disheartening when we read Genesis more closely: Sin was running wild and God was doing some things that don't seem to make sense.

For starters: why would a loving God wipe out 99% of humanity?

In the previous chapter, we learned that God loves us even in the midst of our sinfulness. God's first response to sin was hope. God promised He would one day crush the serpent's head. There would be pain in childbirth, yes; but one day a child would be born to defeat the Evil One. God showed love after our disobedience. But the choice to rebel ruined a world that was "very good."

Children are born, families are formed, and the world keeps spinning. As time moves forward, the roots of sin affix themselves to everything they touch.

"The LORD saw that the wickedness of man was great in the earth, and that every intention of the thoughts of his heart was only evil continually" (Genesis 6:5).

The Bible does not exaggerate things. Genesis 6:5 is not an approximation. People quickly discovered how much they loved sin and self. Great wickedness took over the earth like a ripple on still water shooting outward in every direction. Adam and Eve's choice to rebel against God's rule rippled throughout every future generation. The phrase is haunting: *"every intention* of the thoughts of his heart was only evil *continually."* The writer used the words "every" and "only." There weren't just a few poor choices or small lapses in judgment. The world was continually moving toward evil. Sinfulness was an all-consuming thought. If sin consumed every thought, then it affected every action. There were no other thoughts. Sin wasn't just present, it corrupted everything. It ran wild.

In Romans 1, the Apostle Paul describes sin running wild. The words he uses paint a picture of what was going on in Genesis 6. People took the beauty of God's creation and twisted it into something perverse. Hearts overflowed with murder, envy, and discontent. Maliciousness was served with a side dish of deceit. Humans invented new forms of evil. They were foolish, faithless, and ruthless. They couldn't trust their friends because everyone was an enemy. The corruption of the world was so heinous that it deserved to be destroyed.

Everyone knew of God's creation, power, and eternal nature. They could see it in creation. But instead of worshipping Him, they decided to worship anything and everything else. They celebrated the rejection of their Creator; everyone except Noah. The Bible says, "Noah walked with God" (Genesis 6:9).

Read Genesis 6:8–22.

As we read the Noah story, we find God pushing "reset" on humanity. He chooses one man's family to begin the world again. Noah is counted as righteous and blameless, but Noah isn't perfect. He is not righteous because he is good. Noah's faith finds favor with God. God saves Noah and his family because Noah trusts the Creator.

There were death, unpleasant smells, and mourning for the lost. There was an ocean with no shoreline. Imagine seeing nothing but wave after wave. (I wonder who the first person was to see the mountain peek through the water.) Then a dove arrived with a tree branch in its mouth. Hope sprang to life with the world reborn. Genesis later tells us that "Noah became a man of the soil" (Genesis 9:20). I love this idea: The man who is most famous for being on an ark decided he liked the dirt. (If I never left a giant zoo boat for almost a year, I'd sure consider an occupation away from animals and water!) But before Noah began his life as a farmer, God gave him and his family some assurances. God made a promise.

"The LORD said in his heart, "I will never again curse the ground because of man, for the intention of man's heart is evil from his youth. Neither will I

13

ever again strike down every living creature as I have done. While the earth remains, seedtime and harvest, cold and heat, summer and winter, day and night, shall not cease" (Genesis 8:21, 22).

Even though sin still persisted, God promised to repopulate and redeem His creation through one man. One righteous man started again with faith as his foundation. God sealed him into the ark. The world outside was dying, but God sealed Noah and his family in to be saved; the ark is like a reverse tomb. After the waters receded, God brought Noah out and made a promise: He'll never bring death to the world in this way again. Then God gave Noah a familiar task.

"And you, be fruitful and multiply, increase greatly on the earth and multiply in it." Then God said to Noah and to his sons with him, "Behold, I establish my covenant with you and your offspring after you" (Genesis 9:7–9).

Up to this point in Genesis, we have seen two things: God's faithfulness and our sinfulness. Here, God again called His people to multiply and spread out over all the earth, which is the same command He gave to Adam and Eve: spread out and take over. Mankind heard this, but they still chose their own plans. They were not interested in what God wanted for them.

Noah represents a new start with people who trust God. Noah was over 600 years old after the flood, but his family kept growing. There were more families, more people, and the earth began to be populated again. I would venture to say that more than a few of them heard the flood story because Noah knew God, walked with God, and talked about the things of God. You would think everyone knew what had happened and why.

But then we come to Genesis 11. Close to five centuries had passed since the flood. That's a lot of generations; surely people understood what God had called them to do: fill the earth, spread out, take over, and make the name of God great. But they didn't.

Read Genesis 11:1–9.

Out of context, the story of the tower of Babel can seem perplexing. It almost feels like God was trying to stop progress. People learned how to make bricks and they were working together. There was innovation and achievement. But God was not concerned with bricks. Genesis 11:4 reveals the problem: "Let us build ourselves a city…let us make a name for ourselves." The people wanted so badly to be famous. They wanted to be revered for what they had accomplished.

So God confused their language and spread them out across the earth. Before, God had wiped out the earth because of humanity's direct disobedience. At Babel, God kept His promise and the results still impact us today. War and racism can be traced back to Babel. Noah's family and lineage weren't enough. Sin still ran wild.

———

After sin entered this world, things got messy; and things have never improved. We continue to see both God's faithfulness and man's ability to choose sin and self-destruction.

When I look at my own life, I see this pattern play out again and again. I often find sin running wild in my own life. God made me in His image and called me to make His name great; but I take the gift of life and make it about me. It's *my* life and *my* stuff. They're *my* desires. I understand the desire to make a name for oneself. I can make the good things I do be about me "being good." Sometimes I do good things for selfish reasons. I have no problem being foolish. Anger flares up as easily as a new friendship. I am gifted at judging others. It's so easy for me to see how they should live their lives. I know what they did wrong and how they are going to pay for that mistake. I don't even need to speak directly with them about a situation. I just bang my gavel. Everywhere I look, I see sin running wild in my life.

What's more, I have been betrayed. I have been slandered. People have hated me and talked behind my back. But I've done the same things. I betray. I slander. I have had hatred in my heart and even wished death upon others. And all along the way, I claim to follow God. I'm all over the place.

We are all this way. Sin is running wild.

We can't make up our minds; but God is completely consistent. He doesn't change. His message of multiplication, advancement, and honoring Him is present at both the beginning of creation and after the flood.

God called His creation to live for Him. His children chose to reject Him and live for themselves. Sin ran wild; but all hope was not lost.

Salvation is visible throughout these stories. When God sealed Noah and his family into the ark, He was protecting them. He was saving them from certain death. God saves the righteous. He saves those who believe and trust Him.

In a way, you could say that Noah is a 'reverse' Jesus: one man saved humanity while all the sinful people died. At Babel, we learn that Noah wasn't enough. He was faithful, but he wasn't perfect. Thousands of years later, Jesus will give up His life for all sinners, offering them salvation. What a beautiful picture of God's consistent faithfulness! In God's punishment for sin running wild, He's still pointing to Jesus. One man is chosen to save the world and repopulate it. That man is Noah, who walks with God.

"By faith Noah, being warned by God concerning events as yet unseen, in reverent fear constructed an ark for the saving of his household. By this he condemned the world and became an heir of the righteousness that comes by faith" (Hebrews 11:7).

I think one of the best takeaways from the life of Noah is found in his righteousness. The New Testament writers mention Noah several times as a hero of faith. Noah's acts of goodness did not make him righteous; his complete trust in God did. This is an amazing thing to consider. I'm not sure what I would do if God told me He was going to kill all the living things on earth. God told Noah a flood was coming; but Noah didn't get to see the flood beforehand. Instead, God gave Noah specific instructions for building a giant boat in the middle of dry land. When I put myself in Noah's situation, it's hard for me to know what I would have done.

The faithfulness it took to build an ark without knowing when, or if, the world would flood is remarkable. It's true faith on display. Noah's faith in God was the opposite of the attitude of the rest of the world. While Noah trusted God, sin ran wild in everyone's hearts.

I find great hope in knowing God is not only looking for righteous deeds in my life. God first wants me to trust Him. In the center of this crazy world where sin runs wild, God is completely consistent. He has not changed. He loves and cares for His people by giving them hope that is solely found in Him.

Reflection

Read Genesis 6:5—11:9 again. Take your time. Think about what's been connected so far in God's story of redemption. Slow down; pretend this is the first time you've read this. Think about the words you are reading.

1. Genesis 6:5 says, *"every intention of the thoughts of his heart was only evil continually."* Do you think we face the same situation today? In what ways could you see this world constantly have its heart focused on evil?
2. What do you think were some problems Noah's family faced inside the ark?
3. How does God's promise to Noah show us God's consistency toward humanity?
4. Consider your past. In what ways do you recognize "sin running wild" in your personal history?
5. How has God's faithfulness impacted your spiritual journey?
6. What would the Bible say about your relationship with God? Would it say that you "walked with God"? What can you learn about walking with God from Noah?

CHAPTER 3

A Nobody

After the flood, hundreds of years pass. Generations come forth from the four sons of Noah, and nations are formed. In the future, many of these nations will cause problems for God's people. At this time, as in our own time, only two kinds of people exist in the world: those focused on evil and those found with faith. From Noah's family, there are still righteous men. But there are also people who have formed nations and religions apart from God. Sin is present, but so is faith. After nine generations of fathers, all of whom live several hundred years, we come to the story of Terah, Abram, and Sarai.

We know that Terah had three sons; one of them was Abram. He married Sarai. In the beginning of their story, all we know is that they were unable to have children. They stayed close to Abram's father and his family. Then, something miraculous happened.

"Now the LORD said to Abram, 'Go from your country and your kindred and your father's house to the land that I will show you. And I will make of you a great nation, and I will bless you and make your name great, so that you will be a blessing. I will bless those who bless you, and him who dishonors you I will curse, and in you all the families of the earth shall be blessed.' So Abram went, as the LORD had told him, and Lot went with him. Abram was seventy-five years old when he departed from Haran. And Abram took Sarai his wife, and Lot his brother's son, and all their possessions that they had gathered, and the people that they had acquired in Haran, and they set out to go to the land of Canaan. When they came to the land of Canaan, Abram passed through the land to the place at Shechem, to the oak of Moreh. At that time the Canaanites were in the land. Then the LORD appeared to Abram and said, 'To your offspring I will give this land.' So he built there an altar to the LORD, who had appeared to him"
(Genesis 12:1–7).

God showed up. It's hard to imagine what a shock this would have been. I wonder what Abram was doing. It must have been a normal day; Abram was doing the same thing he always did. Then the Creator of the universe began speaking to him! When the Lord showed up, He made three initial promises to Abram. First, God promised He would bless Abram. Second, God said Abram would become the father of a great nation. Finally, and perhaps most intriguingly, God promised that the entire world would be blessed through Abram and his family. There were three promises: personal blessing, a great nation, and a blessing for the world.

It's funny to me that we know so little about Abram. The only thing we really know flies in the face of God's promises. The man who couldn't have children was about to father a great nation. God promised a family to a 75-year-old man with a barren wife.

Later in Scripture, the Book of Joshua gives a history lesson about this family. Joshua tells us that Abram wasn't even a follower of God; he was an idolater (Joshua 24:2). This means Abram must have abandoned a different religion when he followed God. The father of the entire Hebrew faith, the one God chose to bless, did not even worship the God of Noah. The God of the universe decided to use an old man with no children who didn't even worship Him to be the founder of a blessed nation. God can use anyone.

In Genesis 12:1–7, God appeared to Abram out of nowhere and spoke to him. God said, "Go from your country and your kindred and your father's house to the land that I will show you" (Genesis 12:1). The Lord made a lot of promises, but God never told Abram where he was going! He just said, "Go," and "I will show you." As God revealed Himself to Abram, Abram responded immediately in faith. He spoke to his family, packed everything up, and started walking. I would have loved to have been a fly on the wall for that family meeting. *"Hey everyone, glad you are here, couple of things: Number one, God spoke to me. No, not that one, another one; we'll talk about Him later. Number two, we've got to move; all of us. Get your things together. Where are we going? Oh, He'll tell us later."* There had to be questions and doubt. Nonetheless, they all packed up everything and headed toward a place called Canaan.

Based on the way his family responds, I think it is safe to say they trusted Abram. His extended family was willing to go with him on this journey. His wife packed her belongings and was ready for this new adventure. They must have trusted Abram enough to be willing to follow him as he followed this unknown God.

I am wowed by Abram's faith. At seventy-five, Abram was probably set in his ways. He knew children were off the table. He was probably just fine living in Haran. His family was with him. It's safe to assume Abram was content to settle down for the rest of his life. But one day, the God of creation appeared to him and Abram responded in faith.

In the days of Abram, it had been several hundred years since Noah. Abram likely knew the story of Noah, or at least some version of it. But we do not know whether he knew or had even heard of God. He worshipped family gods. This makes Abram's choice astounding. Abram's actions were based on God's promises. When God called, Abram answered and journeyed with all he possessed to an unknown land: Canaan. Yet another blessing is revealed when they arrive in Canaan; God promised Abram and his descendants that He would give them this land.

Read Genesis 15:1–7.

While Abram is impressive because of his faith, all pales in comparison to what God has done. God created the world and brought a flood. He made plans to repopulate the world through one family. Then, God chooses to do something that appeared undoable. The Lord gave two aging people with no future a blessing of immeasurable proportions. God can do anything. God can use anyone. God's design has purpose far beyond our understanding.

Read Genesis 17:4–8.

About fifteen years later, when Abram was ninety-nine years of age and still childless, God visited him again and made another promise. He also gave him a new name: Abraham, which means "father of a multitude of nations." Sarai, Abraham's wife, became Sarah, which means "princess." Much had happened to Abraham and his family, but God continued to provide for them. The blessing of land was given, and the personal blessing was evident in many ways. But life was not easy, nor exactly as they expected.

Several years passed and Sarai was still without child. How could there be a great nation with no child? At one point, Sarah even laughed at the thought of being pregnant at such an old age. God's response to her laughter is recorded in Genesis 18:14:

"Is anything too hard for the LORD? At the appointed time I will return to you, about this time next year, and Sarah shall have a son."

One year later, twenty-five years after God made His promises to Abram, Sarah became pregnant. She gave birth to a boy named Isaac. Two of the four promises were met. Abraham was blessed and the hope for a future nation was fulfilled.

God's blessing goes forward from Abraham to his son Isaac. Isaac's son, Jacob, births a nation. His twelve sons become twelve tribes who become the nation of Israel. This all comes from two nobodies who came from nowhere, didn't know God, and weren't able to have children. God can do anything. God can use anyone. Nothing is too difficult for Him.

———

The story of Abraham almost seems fantastical. God appeared to him, his whole understanding of things changed, and he received blessing beyond belief.

As other-worldly as Abraham's story is, it is grounded in real problems. Abram and Sarai couldn't have children. They were just trying to survive in the day-to-day. We can relate to a life like that. But we can also learn from Abraham and Sarah. From them, we learn God can use anyone, we can respond to God's call, and God can do anything.

It does not matter where you come from. You could have been a drug addict, Girl Scout, politician, engineer, full-time mom, or reality TV star before your life of faith. It doesn't matter who you've been or from where you've come. God selected Abram . . . and Abram was a whole lot of unimportant.

I come from a good family. They encouraged, loved, and cared for me as a young man. There is nothing special about my upbringing or lineage. It is special to me, but I'm no one extraordinary. Maybe that is your story too.

Here's the wonderful thing we see in Abraham's story: God can use anyone for His purposes and glory. Abram worshipped other gods. It is possible that you have worshipped other things in your life (I know I have). God can still use you. It doesn't matter how bad you've been or how undeserving you are, God still wants you to know Him. God wants you to have a relationship with Him. God appeared to you through Jesus Christ. God can use anyone and has revealed Himself to everyone through Christ.

God also gives us opportunities to respond in faith. Just like Abram, we have no idea what is going to happen in our lives. The future is uncertain to us. Yet we know the author of our future. Abram didn't know everything, he just believed God. Abram's belief led him to follow God's call. We have the same opportunity to trust God with our future. Wherever we go, whatever we do, God is calling us to live for Him.

We should not hesitate to compare our lives to Abraham. He was far from perfect and made lots of mistakes. Yet when you look at the totality of his life, you see a pattern of faithfulness. If God called you today to follow Him, what would you do? Would you be willing to pack up everything you have, tell your family what God has said, and ask them to join you in a journey of faith?

I want to be like Abraham. I want to listen to God's truth and respond with a life of faithfulness.

Our reason for a life of faith comes from the simple fact that God is capable of anything. Nothing is impossible for God. I have seen God move in power. As a minister, I have seen first-hand the saving power of Jesus Christ. I know men and women who are different people because of their trust in God. They no longer live for themselves, but have answered God's call in their lives. I have watched marriages be pieced back together by forgiveness and grace. I know people who should be dead, but God has healed them. I have seen money show up just as it was needed. I know people who are going through the worst moments of their lives, yet God is bringing comfort. I have watched God bring mercy to the hurting. I have seen so many tangible examples of His love. I know God can do anything for His glory.

It's hard to believe Sarah had a baby when she was 100 years old. That is something only God can do. They had the promise of land, they had a son, and they had a future. But how do you go from a small family to a nation that will impact the future of the world forever? This seems extremely difficult. A new nation seems fragile. It would need supreme protection to turn into something through which God could bless the world, particularly when you consider how many times Abraham and his own family acted contrary to the promises.

Abraham's grandson, Jacob, had some sons who could not get along. All the brothers hated their younger brother, Joseph. They ended up selling him as a slave to Egypt. In Egypt, Joseph became second in command of the greatest civilization at that time. This all happened during a time of a severe drought and famine, the very thing that could destroy the promise of a nation. But by God's design, Joseph was able to protect the people of God. Look at what Joseph said about his brothers in Genesis 50:20:

> *"As for you, you meant evil against me, but God meant it for good, to bring it about that many people should be kept alive, as they are today."*

Abraham's family went to live with Joseph under the protection of Egypt. God allowed them to prosper.

> *"Then Joseph died, and all his brothers and all that generation. But the people of Israel were fruitful and increased greatly; they multiplied and grew exceedingly strong, so that the land was filled with them"* (Exodus 1:6, 7).

Abraham's family had grown. They would soon have a land of their own and be a great nation. Only one promise was left: that the whole earth will be blessed through Abraham's offspring.

Jesus is all over the story of Abraham. When we think about the birth of Jesus, it reminds us of Sarah. Sarah could not have a child; she was barren. Mary had never been with a man before, so there is no way she could be pregnant. But nothing is impossible for God.

The pregnancy of Sarah and Abraham birthed Isaac. From Isaac came generation after generation of God's protection and blessing of His people. The promise that "in you all the families of the earth shall be blessed," is fulfilled in Jesus Christ (Genesis 12:3). The lineage of Jesus can be traced all the way back to Abraham.

Thousands of years after Abraham lived, a baby would be born in Bethlehem; He would be from the offspring of Eve through the line of Abraham. He would ultimately crush the head of the serpent in the most unexpected way.

From Sarah to Mary, we see God doing things that can't be done. Nothing is impossible for God.

Reflection

Read Genesis 12:1–7, 15:3–6, and 17:4–8 again. Take your time. Think about what's been connected so far in God's story of redemption. Slow down; pretend this is the first time you've read this. Think about the words you are reading.

1. Compare Noah's faith to Abraham's faith. After Noah, there were more faithful people on Earth. How does Noah's righteous lineage reveal itself in Abraham's choices?
2. How is Abraham's reaction to God's call significant to his story of redemption?
3. Write down a few moments from the stories of Noah, Abraham, and Joseph through which God's creativity in keeping His promises has overwhelmed you.
4. Reflect upon your own conversion. When did God speak to you? When was the first time you chose to follow Jesus with your life?
5. What are some moments in your past when you can see your steps of faith impacting your future?
6. Prayerfully consider all the ways God has done impossible things in your life.

CHAPTER 4

I AM

400 years passed from the time of Joseph to the time of Moses. Joseph had done great things for the people of Egypt, but Egypt eventually became concerned and uncomfortable with his descendants.

"Now there arose a new king over Egypt, who did not know Joseph. And he said to his people, 'Behold, the people of Israel are too many and too mighty for us. Come, let us deal shrewdly with them, lest they multiply, and, if war breaks out, they join our enemies and fight against us and escape from the land'" (Exodus 1:8–10).

God was building a nation. Generations after Isaac, Abraham's family was growing immensely. Egypt was worried. Abraham's nation, which God promised to bless, was forced into oppression and slavery. The growth continued, and Egypt's fear grew to the point that they started killing Hebrew children.

Read Exodus 2.

Moses began his life under God's blessing and protection. God had a special plan for Moses. He was born a slave, only to be adopted into the house of Pharaoh himself. He became a prince of Egypt. But the prince could not run from his Hebrew heritage; the plight of his people was too much for him. After killing a slave taskmaster, Moses became a fugitive. He escaped to the wilderness to hide. There, far away from both Egypt and Israel, Moses married and became a shepherd.

Many years after the palaces of Egypt and the life he once knew, Moses found himself standing on the side of a mountain, staring at a bush that was burning, but not on fire. The same God who spoke to Abraham also spoke to Moses.

"Then the LORD said, 'I have surely seen the affliction of my people who are in Egypt and have heard their cry because of their taskmasters. I know their sufferings, and I have come down to deliver them out of the hand of the Egyptians'" (Exodus 3:7, 8).

God spoke to Moses. He had seen, heard, and knew His people's suffering. The time had come for God to deliver His people, and He wanted to send Moses as His messenger. Among the many startling questions Moses had, I find one to be the most shocking. In Exodus 3:13, 14, Moses literally asks God who He is:

"Then Moses said to God, 'If I come to the people of Israel and say to them, 'The God of your fathers has sent me to you,' and they ask me, 'What is his name?' what shall I say to them?' God said to Moses, 'I AM WHO I AM.' And he said, 'Say this to the people of Israel: 'I AM has sent me to you.''"

In this moment, God revealed Himself to the very people He had promised to make into a great nation. Think about this: They didn't know His name. I grew up in church. I knew what to call God at an early age. The Israelites, however, knew very little about who

God is. All they knew was what Abraham had passed down and what their parents taught them from the stories of Joseph. It had been 400 years, and the only thing they had experienced was suffering. God finally showed up to save them, but who was He? *"I AM WHO I AM."* There had to be doubts and questions.

We must not forget, in this moment, the God of the universe is re-introducing Himself to the people He promised to bless. He is re-introducing Himself to Moses, Egypt, and the rest of the known world. *I AM* has shown up. This name is an answer involving space, time, and existence. God is present. God has been with them all along. He is moving in power for their release. This God is real, He is here, and He is with them.

The deliverance of Israel was quite the re-introduction. God put on a show of power and might. Egypt worshipped many gods. They had idols, statues, and temples. Pharaoh himself was considered a god. One by one, the God of Israel defeated every Egyptian god. God sent plagues and each one decimated one of Egypt's false gods. Egypt worshiped their river; they saw the great Nile turn to blood. Egypt had harvest gods; swarms of animals and insects destroyed their crops and brought disease. Physical ailments such as boils afflicted the people, overcoming the Egyptian gods of medicine and peace. Lastly, the son of Pharaoh was killed. None of their gods compared to *I AM*[1].

Moses finally led the people of Israel out of Egypt, but it was clear he wasn't the one leading. He followed a supernatural pillar of cloud by day and fire by night. The pillar from God led them indirectly back to the place where Moses first saw the bush that didn't burn up. This was the place where God formally re-introduced Himself to the Israelites.

"While Moses went up to God. The LORD called to him out of the mountain, saying, 'Thus you shall say to the house of Jacob, and tell the people of Israel: 'You yourselves have seen what I did to the Egyptians, and how I bore you on eagles' wings and brought you to myself. Now therefore, if you will indeed obey my voice and keep my covenant, you shall be my

treasured possession among all peoples, for all the earth is mine; and you shall be to me a kingdom of priests and a holy nation'" (Exodus 19:3–6).

God kept every promise He had made to Noah, Abraham, and Moses. At this point, Exodus 19 tells of a covenant promise between God and the people of Israel. Moses told them what God said and they were to respond. God reminded them that He had delivered them from bondage in Egypt; He then made them a promise of national blessing. God basically said He would make them an example for the world to see, if they would listen and obey (Exodus 19:5). God wanted Israel to know Him and He wanted the world to understand Him. He planned to do this through Israel.

While most nations at that time had a king, God wanted Israel to be different. He wanted them to be a nation of priests. God wanted His people to be intent on serving Him in unity. The entire nation would be set apart for the world to see.

God began by laying out the Ten Commandments.

Read Exodus 20:1–21.

After having a front row seat to the humiliation of Egypt, the parting of the Red Sea, and a mountain shaking with thunder and lightning, the first few commandments were probably not hard for the Hebrews to accept. Of course there should be no other gods before Him. Moses said they should never even use God's name in vain. Makes sense. These are all reminders of God's complete authority and power. He had already shown that He is completely "other" in every sense of the word. These first commandments were the ground rules on how they should think, speak, and operate in reference to God. They had an up-close experience with *I AM WHO I AM*. They were being taught how to relate to Him.

The next several rules all revolved around the way they should treat each other in response to who God is. Rest, honor your parents, do not murder, do not commit adultery, do not steal, do not lie, and don't covet. Setting aside the practical value of every one of these rules, each command makes a statement about the condition of a person's heart.

If you don't rest, you'll have issues with control. Dishonoring your parents exposes your selfishness. The remaining relational laws reveal a personal desire to play god. They all point to the idea that you value yourself more than anyone else. The laws God established can be placed into two categories: love for God and love for others.

There was a great ceremony that is detailed in Exodus 23 and 24. All of Israel was there. Moses did exactly what God asked Him to do. Israel heard what God asked of them; their response was agreeing to do "All the words that the LORD has spoken" (Exodus 24:3).

This didn't last very long. Moses climbed the mountain to receive the laws from God and learn how Israel would operate as a nation. God gave Israel these laws so other nations could know God's character through Israel's example. Moses took longer to come down from the mountain than the Israelites anticipated. So God's chosen nation ran back to their old ways. They made a golden idol and started worshipping it. As quickly as they promised God to love and follow Him, they went straight back to the old and false gods.

God had delivered them. God had revealed Himself to them. God had shown them His great plan for the world, but they decided to live for themselves. They chose a path of sin and selfishness over the promise they had made to live for God. (This sounds a lot like two people living in paradise deciding they would eat from a forbidden tree.)

In the middle of this sadness, I find great hope in how Moses responds to God. Moses had spent more time with God than Israel had. He had listened to everything God had said and promised.

Moses started his journey in fear; he wasn't even sure who was talking to him. He started by having to ask God His name. At this moment, when Israel had sinned against God, Moses spoke words of forgiveness and hope. Moses offered his own life for the people of Israel.

"The next day Moses said to the people, 'You have sinned a great sin. And now I will go up to the LORD; perhaps I can make atonement for your sin.' So Moses returned to the LORD and said, 'Alas, this people has sinned a great sin. They have made for themselves gods of gold. But now, if you will forgive their sin—but if not, please blot me out of your book that you have written.' But the LORD said to Moses, 'Whoever has sinned against me, I will blot out of my book.'" (Exodus 32:30–33).

The cost of sin is death. Moses understood God's holiness and requirement for justice. Moses had learned about God and how to have a relationship with Him. Moses spoke the words of God back to God. He knew the things God cared about. In Exodus 32:32, Moses offered his life in place of Israel. You could read it to say, "Take my life as a sacrifice for their sins." God's response was interesting. He essentially told Moses that his offer was correct, but it wasn't enough. Everyone who sins deserves death.

In Exodus, Leviticus, and Numbers, God established a sacrificial offering system to pay for the sins of Israel. This system required Israel to give up their choicest animals. The animals had to be spotless. (This was an expensive lesson for the people of Israel. A spotless animal was great for breeding or selling. It could have created a continuous source of income.) A priest was to kill the animal and pour the blood over an altar, symbolic of the presence of God. Only when costly blood was spilled and poured out were the people's sins forgiven. God called His people to make a costly sacrifice to renew their relationship with Him.

As God's great story moves forward, Israel, after many acts of rebellion, made it to the land of promise. God went with them. He continued to provide and protect them even though they didn't deserve it. God showed His steadfast love by keeping His promise to Abraham; Israel became a great nation.

God's great plan spans thousands of years and endless stories of His supreme faithfulness. Nothing happens by coincidence or accident. God foreshadows His salvation through His perfect design. In this story, God reveals His power and greatness to a nation that belongs to Him. God instructs them in how they should relate to Him and to one another. But the covenant promise is something Israel cannot keep on its own. They are going to need help. They'll need someone to save them. Moses isn't enough. Joshua won't be either.

———

The story of Moses and the people of Israel teaches us a great deal about God and ourselves. It's a big revelation. God is "*I AM WHO I AM.*" He reveals His purpose, existence, and presence with this one simple phrase. The God who created all things is with us. He is present in our lives. He does not need us. He is. God knows that we need His deliverance. That is why He revealed Himself to Moses, to the people of Israel, and now to us.

The Ten Commandments help us to know God and live in harmony with others. These laws are timeless and true. Beyond showing us how to live, God's laws expose the reality of our spiritual condition. Paul says that "by works of the law no human being will be justified in [God's] sight, since through the law comes knowledge of sin" (Romans 3:20).

These Old Testament laws reveal our need for salvation. The law shows us that we can't keep our promises to God. Just like the Israelites, we can't keep our end of the bargain. We want to do things that make us feel good about ourselves. We worship lots of things that are not God. Most of the time, we are just like Israel. We feel like God is on top of a mountain, not moving fast enough for us. We are wrong, lost, and in need of salvation.

It is truly beautiful that God sees, hears, and knows our sin problem. The people of Israel had Moses who tried to step in and offer his life for theirs. But he wasn't enough. God instituted a sacrificial system to bring the people back to a relationship with Him, but it wasn't lasting. A costly sacrifice needed to be made regularly to make things right. Even these regular sacrifices could never truly atone for our sins.

In God's glorious design, Jesus Christ, the Son of God, is the perfect answer to our sin problem. Jesus was perfectly righteous according to God's law. He never sinned. When Jesus gave up His perfect life, He did what Moses and the animal sacrifices could not. Jesus was a faultless version of Moses. Jesus was the ultimate sacrificial offering. His perfect blood fulfilled God's justice requirement. What Jesus did on the cross is the culmination of everything God did for Israel in Egypt. Jesus is our true deliverance.

I love that God wants us to know Him. He isn't secretive about His revelation. Empires have crumbled and entire seas have parted just to show the glory of God.

I am constantly reminded that God doesn't choose His people and leaders based on ability. God's story is not an accident, but a grand design that points to His hope for humanity through Jesus Christ. God wants us to know Him. He wants us to trust Him. He wants to save us from ourselves. His plan with Moses was to point us to Jesus.

Reflection

Read Exodus, chapters 1—3, 19, 20, and 32, 33 again. Take your time. Think about what's been connected so far in God's story of redemption. Slow down; pretend this is the first time you've read this. Think about the words you are reading.

1. How does God's deliverance of Israel keep the promises He made to Abraham?
2. In what ways do you learn more about God from the Ten Commandments? What do these commands reveal about your choices?
3. Moses uses God's words to defend the people of Israel. Why does he attempt to save them from God's justice?
4. Consider the promises you have in Christ Jesus. How does God's faithfulness bring you encouragement today?
5. Write down a few ways you can love God and others through your obedience to God's laws.
6. Moses knew God's words. How can Scripture memory (speaking God's words) strengthen your prayer life?

CHAPTER 5

Not Enough

God is not enough. At least, that's what Israel believed.

This seems to become a recurring theme in the early stages of Israel developing into a nation. After God wiped out Egypt, Moses left the people for a little longer than expected. Out of fear, Israel turned back to idol worship! As Israel stood outside the borders of the Promised Land, they sent spies into the land to discover what they were up against. When the spies returned, most of them reported that the land was filled with mighty people who could easily overtake Israel. Only two of the spies, Joshua and Caleb, believed God would bring victory. They were ignored and everyone became terrified. The same people who watched God destroy Egypt's army with the Red Sea couldn't imagine a scenario where God defeats a few fortified cities. In their minds, God was not enough for their concerns and fears.

Because of Israel's lack of faith, everyone older than Joshua and Caleb failed to inherit the land promised to them. Their doubt and fears ruined their chances of seeing God move in power.

During forty years of wandering in the wilderness, Moses made one bad choice. He directly disobeyed God's instructions. Due to his disobedience, Moses was also not allowed to enter God's Promised Land. Joshua was chosen to lead the people of Israel into the land flowing with milk and honey.

Through God's design, Moses re-introduced the God of the universe to Abraham's family. Many signs and wonders took place. The time came for Moses to move aside and Joshua to take the lead. Joshua had some big shoes to fill. It would be natural to have some apprehension. The first chapter of Joshua tells us God's instructions to Joshua as he prepared to accept the task before him.

Read Joshua 1.

The same God who remained faithful to Noah, Abraham, Joseph, and Moses encouraged Joshua. Those fortified city walls the people of Israel were so worried about a few decades earlier? They fell down with a little marching and yelling. No battle even took place! God instructed Joshua's people to march around the city walls for six days in a row. On the seventh day, they were to blow trumpets and shout (Joshua 6:5). This was God's plan: marching, trumpets, and shouting. But everything happened just as God promised. The city of Jericho, a part of the Promised Land, was given over to Israel.

Joshua lived a long and faithful life. He led Israel well. Toward the end of his life, Joshua called the people of God together and spoke to them. He asked them to keep trusting God. Joshua told Israel to "cling to the LORD your God just as you have done to this day. For the LORD has driven out before you great and strong nations. And as for you, no man has been able to stand before you to this day" (Joshua 23:8, 9).

Israel was called to drive the other people groups out of the land that was promised to them. Removing people from the same land as Israel was not a form of cruelty, but a necessity. God had called Israel to be different from the rest of the world. Their nation was supposed to resemble a kingdom of priests: an entire group of people committed only to the God of the universe. He called them to drive out the nations that were occupying the land. This was intended to establish a clear picture of God's leadership of Israel. God had called them to be purely focused on Him; but He knew Israel's weaknesses. There were other nations waiting to invite Israel into their pagan lifestyles. God wanted Israel to remain separate, but this did not happen. Little by little, Israel chose to live alongside the different people groups. They bought into false religions and returned to their old ways of life. Israel started to act like the other nations because they longed to be like them.

Israel began to adopt every other religion they could find. They started following false gods that involved fertility, farming, and family. It didn't really matter; if another country worshipped it, Israel was into it. It's ironic to think that other nations were probably jealous of Israel's God. They probably wished their gods would drop food onto the ground for them to eat. They wished their gods would provide for them the way the Lord had done for Israel. However, Israel wanted to be like all the other nations. God let them reap all the consequences of their choices. All the problems that came along with idol worship and corrupt living brought pain and suffering to Israel. Even so, God had mercy on them.

He provided judges—leaders who provided protection and leadership whenever Israel would cry out to God. They helped Israel, but they didn't rule. Part of the reason for the judges was that Israel did not have a king. God was their leader and they were a kingdom of people solely committed to God. This was how it was supposed to be. A king would be like a pharaoh and oppression would certainly follow.

God wanted Israel to be an example to the world of His goodness, but Israel just wanted to be like everyone else. Judges 2:17 gives a graphic description of Israel's actions: "Yet they did not listen to their judges, for they whored after other gods and bowed down to them." God wasn't enough for them. They wanted something else. They wanted anything but God. They would rather have a pharaoh again. They saw other nations with kings and idols, and this is what they wanted.

The Hebrews wanted comfort. They wanted easy lives in which they could do what they wanted, with whom they wanted. Life with God involved rules and a relationship with Him. Israel wanted something easier. They wanted a king.

One of the last judges was a man named Samuel. He was faithful and honored God, but his children did not follow in his footsteps. Samuel's sons became judges, but quickly ruined their reputations by taking bribes and corrupting justice. Israel wanted a new direction.

Read 1 Samuel 8:4–22.

Samuel introduced the time of 1 and 2 Kings. This part of history only occurs because God gave in to what the people wanted for themselves. It is hard to imagine ever saying, "Please oppress me," but that is essentially what Israel asked for. Israel pleaded with Samuel to take their wealth, independence, and children if it meant they could have a king like everyone else.

——

There are some parts of the Scripture that I relate to easily, but this section of history is difficult for me. At first glance, it appears to be a bunch of short-sighted children chasing their immediate desires. I find it hard to relate to full-blown idol worship. After all, the "gods" are made by people! The desire to have a physical king to look up to seems frustratingly unnecessary. But sadly, this time for Israel is more similar to my current life than I would like to admit.

I want my life to be perfect, free from pain and suffering. I want the temperature at my house to be set specifically to my liking. If my clothes aren't comfortable enough, I will go buy more. I want to eat exactly what I crave as soon as the craving hits. I want what I want when I want it.

I may not bow down to a shrine in the corner of my house, but I hold on to my smart phone like it is a lifeline to enlightenment. I stare at the screen as if I am receiving nourishment. When it isn't close by, I reach for it and wonder who may have messaged me.

While my country may not have a king, I worship fame. I am unfortunately aware of many intimate details of complete and total strangers who have somehow obtained celebrity status. Athletes have every moment of their lives recorded for my viewing. I end up knowing everything about them. This makes me a worshipper. The saddest thing about all of this is how my attention can be sold so easily to the highest bidder. Much like Israel, I whore after other gods, chasing pleasure. I wish I couldn't relate to Israel at all, but when I read the book of Judges, I am staring into a mirror.

Israel was jealous of other nations. They looked across the fence and saw palaces, parades, and estates. It felt as if all they had was a bunch of laws that must be followed precisely; failing to do so meant they could die. A king was something you could see. A king could physically pat you on the shoulder as he strolled by. He was not a cloud, a mist, or a fire. He wouldn't speak to a prophet who would then speak to you. He could stand in front of you as a representation of all that was good in your kingdom. A king would be a person you could understand. Understanding God felt much more difficult.

Jealousy is a powerful motivator. It is easy to look across the fence and compare your life with a neighbor's. Their life seems charmed, almost easier. There's never a weed on the front lawn. Their perfectly behaved children always call you "ma'am" or "sir" as they walk their dog that doesn't shed. They got a job promotion, while you don't even get a cost of living increase. The husband and wife share a lingering kiss every morning as they prepare to start their day. Everything just looks easier for them—a wrinkle-free existence—but your life is a struggle. You find yourself wishing just one thing would go your way. We can be much like the child who wishes for divorced parents so they can have two Christmases. More presents sound good, but at what cost?

Israel had the Creator on their side, but they were jealous of the other nations. They thought the lives of others were easier. So, God gave the people what they wanted. Sadly, it was far from what they needed. They chose man over God. God allowed this to happen. (This is a choice that we still make today.) Not only does God know what is best for His people, but He clearly told them what to do. There was no confusion about God's message. Sadly, there was no confusion on where Israel stood either. They wanted their way. God allowed it to happen. God's chosen people did not choose God. They wanted a man to lead them.

The Bible is not a textbook. It is a message breathed out by God. God's story reveals His nature and ours. Mankind repeatedly tells God that He is not enough; Israel sought something different than their Lord. Rather than choosing to destroy Israel, God showed pity and unconditional love during the time of Judges and Kings.

It could be easy to read this story and think that God's plan didn't work. He wanted the world to see Him through His relationship with Israel. Even though Israel was unfaithful, the world still saw a faithful God. That was His plan. God revealed His unwavering love and mercy to people who did not deserve it.

The thing is, Abram didn't deserve God's love and mercy either. The only thing that set him apart was the thing that set Noah apart: *faith*. When God spoke to both of these men, they believed Him and acted. In both cases, God's blessing was undeserved. God's love cannot be matched. His patient caring and gentleness to those who actively rejected Him is unthinkable. This was God's plan— His design.

Israel told God that He wasn't enough. They looked for salvation elsewhere. They did not recognize the truth that no judge or king can save; only God can. Judges and kings aren't enough; only God is enough. In a way, we can see pale comparisons to Jesus in this story. We see judges who tried to step in and lead God's people, just as Jesus will lead, but they fell short. We are introduced to kings who ruled by God's power, but unlike Jesus, they got wrapped up in their majesty more than God's might.

You and I also look to things other than Jesus to save us. We think more knowledge and understanding is what we need. We think that more money or prestige will help buy our salvation. We think that technology will cure disease and solve hunger. We are no different than Israel; we are more than willing to put our faith in everything else but Jesus.

When Jesus comes, He will be Israel's righteous Judge. Jesus is the eternal King. He is the Messiah Israel and the world needs. Jesus is the only King worthy of the throne.

The truth is that *we* are not enough. If we have sinned at all, no amount of goodness can bring salvation. Jesus is our righteous Judge. Jesus is our eternal King. Jesus is the Messiah we need. The only thing that will satisfy the justice of God is a perfect sacrifice. Jesus is enough.

Reflection

Read Joshua 1, Judges 2, and 1 Samuel 8 again. Take your time. Think about what's been connected so far in God's story of redemption. Slow down; pretend this is the first time you've read this. Think about the words you are reading.

1. What examples of God's consistency do you see in Joshua 1?
2. How did Israel rebel against God in Judges 2?
3. Count the ways that Israel told Samuel God wasn't enough for them in 1 Samuel 8.
4. How does God's faithfulness to His people give you the courage to live for Him today?
5. Part of the reason Israel ran from God was because they didn't know Him. How can you grow in your understanding of God?
6. Name a few ways you can fight idolatry in your life. How can you actively choose to live for Christ?

CHAPTER 6

Crumbled Kingdom

"Cling to the Lord." That was one of the last things Joshua said to the people of Israel (Joshua 23:8). It was a call to remember what God had done, and to trust in Him for strength. But Israel did not listen. In their minds, God wasn't enough for them. They wanted what all the other nations had—a king for their kingdom.

The prophet and judge Samuel gave Israel a warning about kings: God would give them a king, but it would essentially return them to slavery and servitude. Joshua used the word "cling," but the response of Israel to the Lord was more akin to "repel." They tried to do whatever they could to *repel* the things of God. Israel went from a kingdom of priests called to serve God to a kingdom with an earthly king. It didn't go very well.

Saul, David, and Solomon were three of Israel's most famous kings. Saul was the first.

1 Samuel 10:17–27 tells the coronation of Israel's first king. Everyone came from far away to discover who would be the new monarch. Saul was everything Israel was looking for: he was handsome and a full head taller than other men (1 Samuel 9:2). However, when they went to select Saul as king, he was hiding among everyone's luggage! Saul was a "nobody" who came from one of the smallest tribes of Israel. However, when the people saw how impressive he looked, shouts of "Long live the king" rang out. (This sounds much like picking a surgeon based on his "kind eyes.") It was not a promising start.

Read 1 Samuel 15.

Israel had a king, but God was still in charge. Saul had a few great military victories and enjoyed the benefits of being king. The longer he stayed king, the less he wanted to be told what to do—He began to pay less and less attention to God's orders. God was clear: wipe out the Amalekites. They were a wicked people who had done many horrible things to Israel. Saul defeated the Amalekites in battle, but decided to keep King Agag alive. He also wanted the Amalekites' best cattle. Saul wanted more than God's favor, he also wanted the best of everything else. Because Saul blatantly disobeyed, God rejected him as king. God told Saul that "to obey is better than sacrifice" (1 Samuel 15:22).

After this, the prophet Samuel set out to discover God's next king for Israel. God directed him to the house of Jesse. One at a time, Samuel met Jesse's sons. His oldest son appeared "kingly," but God told Samuel to "not look on his appearance or on the height of his stature, because I have rejected him. For the LORD sees not as man sees: man looks on the outward appearance, but the LORD looks on the heart" (1 Samuel 16:7). Seven sons were paraded before Samuel; none of them were the right man for the job. Samuel asked if there were any other sons. He was told that the youngest, David, was out tending sheep. Samuel found David and

48

anointed him as the future king right then and there! God had chosen a man after His own heart.

David was a great king. He loved God. After many military victories and honoring God with His choices, David wanted to build a house for God. God's response was epic in proportion.

Read 2 Samuel 7:4–17.

According to God's instruction, Moses had built a tent to represent God's throne room. It was a temple, of sorts. This tent was the place God's Spirit resided. Wherever the Israelites traveled, the tent (tabernacle) was placed in the center of camp. This tent lasted until the time of David; to David, it no longer seemed enough.

An example of David's love for God was when he said, "God, I want to build you a house!" God responded to David with the idea of building something with eternal value. He replied, "No. I am going to build *your house!*" God told David, "Your throne shall be established forever" (2 Samuel 7:16)! David knew of Abraham's blessing. Amazingly, God also made a promise to *him!* God declared that David's house and reign would be forever, and vowed that an eternal Savior-King would arise through David's offspring.

After this blessing, David grew tired of going off to battle as king. In 2 Samuel, chapters 11 and 12, David found himself in the wrong place at the wrong time. When he should have been off to war, he was home gazing outdoors. He discovered a woman bathing on a rooftop. He lusted after the married woman and eventually slept with her. This abuse of power caused her to be pregnant. David schemed to cover up her pregnancy; this eventually led to the murder of the woman's husband. The sin of disobedience in David's heart and mind progressed to the sin of murder. Absolute power caused King David trouble, just as it had for Saul.

This trend toward being corrupted by power did not change as the throne passed to the next generation.

David's son Solomon became king. Solomon was the greatest king Israel would know. Under Solomon's leadership, Israel became greater than every other nation on earth. He led the nation to intellectual advancements, engineering feats, and the accumulation of wealth beyond anything the world had never seen. All his success stemmed from one moment. Much like his father David, Solomon loved the Lord and followed God. In a dream, God came to Solomon and offered him a blessing. Solomon's request allowed Israel to succeed like never before.

Read 1 Kings 3:3–14.

Solomon tasted success like no one else. He built the temple that David wanted for God. He built palaces. The book of 1 Kings is quite detailed about Solomon's blessings. His wealth was not his downfall. Sadly, Solomon's love for sex corrupted his devotion to God. Through his relationships, Solomon allowed other religions into Israel.

Read 1 Kings 11:1–10.

Solomon had 700 wives and 300 concubines. These women came from all over the world, bringing along all sorts of false religions. The Bible says that "Solomon clung to these in love" (1 Kings 11:2). Joshua told the Israelites to cling to the Lord, but Solomon chose to cling to desire. This lust moved his heart away from the things of God. Solomon even built places of worship for other gods; these pagan temples existed inside the nation that was called to be a kingdom of priests for God.

"Therefore the LORD said to Solomon, "Since this has been your practice and you have not kept my covenant and my statutes that I have commanded you, I will surely tear the kingdom from you and will give it to your servant. Yet for the sake of David your father I will not do it in your days, but I will tear it out of the hand of your son. However, I will not tear away all the

50

kingdom, but I will give one tribe to your son, for the sake of David my
servant and for the sake of Jerusalem that I have chosen"
(1 Kings 11:11–13).

It is startling to think that a man who clearly knew God and lived for Him could fall so far. In his old age, Solomon turned his heart away from God and toward false things. God tore Israel in half because of Solomon's wicked behavior. Everything that was built began to crack. Solomon's reign lasted forty years. When he died, his son, Rehoboam, became king. Rehoboam's rule was far different from that of Solomon and David.

Read 1 Kings 12:1–24.

The new king decided to do things his way in this divided kingdom. Rehoboam had a chance to do well. The people said, "Less taxation. Be a good king." Rehoboam thought about it. He went and talked to advisers. They told him, "If you do well and listen, the people will love you forever." His response was, "You think my father was tough, I'm going to be even worse!"

This direction resulted in Rehoboam losing half the nation. The Northern Kingdom, Israel, took Jeroboam as king. The Southern Kingdom was named Judah and was still led by Rehoboam.

King Jeroboam didn't want his people to defect to the Southern Kingdom, so he made them golden calves to worship (1 Kings 12:28). It is almost like he went back in time to pick the wickedest thing he could find with which to tempt his people.

Both kingdoms continued to stray further and further from God. Years later, the prophet Micah described the state of the kingdoms:

"Hear this, you heads of the house of Jacob and rulers of the house of Israel,
who detest justice and make crooked all that is straight, who build Zion with
blood and Jerusalem with iniquity. Its heads give judgment for a bribe; its
priests teach for a price; its prophets practice divination for money; yet they

lean on the LORD and say, 'Is not the LORD in the midst of us? No disaster shall come upon us.' Therefore because of you Zion shall be plowed as a field; Jerusalem shall become a heap of ruins, and the mountain of the house a wooded height" (Micah 3:9–12).

The people of both kingdoms experienced rampant wickedness and corruption. Both governments chose money over justice; the priests accepted bribes for God's "blessing." God's people had abandoned His design. They didn't honor the Sabbath. They had no honor for their parents. Adultery was prevalent. Officials and leaders were guilty of stealing, lying, and coveting.

It is unsettling to consider all that induced God's decision to topple the nation He built. All the things that God had set forth for them in the Ten Commandments had failed. They weren't treating each other right. Moreover, God's chosen people were actively choosing to worship other gods. God watched His people choose a king over Him; then they chose other gods. Because of such blatant disobedience, the kingdoms fell.

"In the ninth year of Hoshea, the king of Assyria captured Samaria, and he carried the Israelites away to Assyria and placed them in Halah, and on the Habor, the river of Gozan, and in the cities of the Medes. Israel fell. And this occurred because the people of Israel had sinned against the LORD their God, who had brought them up out of the land of Egypt from under the hand of Pharaoh king of Egypt, and had feared other gods and walked in the customs of the nations whom the LORD drove out before the people of Israel, and in the customs that the kings of Israel had practiced" (2 Kings 17:6–9).

The king of Assyria not only defeated and captured the Southern Kingdom, he scattered the people of Israel all over the earth. The Northern Kingdom fell just as quickly.

Read 2 Kings 25:1–7.

This was a dark time in the history of God's people. Though Israel was selfishly disobeying God, God never wavered in His promise.

Israel became a nation, only to be split, conquered, and scattered. Yet God's faithfulness remained.

It's a little overwhelming, but Jesus told a parable that reminds me of God's consistent faithfulness during Israel's many times of rebelling.

Read Luke 15:11–32.

A son told his father to give him his inheritance early. That's like saying, "Dad, I want you to die now, so I can have your money for myself." He wanted all the blessing, but none of the responsibility to honor his father. That son went and did whatever he wanted with whomever he wanted; he totally squandered his inheritance and blessing. He finally found himself sitting in the filth of a pig pen. The image of his father looking across the horizon waiting for his son to return is heart-wrenching.

Israel was a prodigal nation and God was a faithful, loving father. In this dark moment in Hebrew history, God's people were fallen, trampled, and scattered; they were an entire people group sitting in slop.

During this time of crumbled kingdoms, God continued to protect Israel in unique ways. He saved faithful men from a fiery furnace. He blessed Daniel and protected him in a den of lions. He took a young Hebrew woman named Esther and made her the queen of a pagan kingdom to protect Israel's scattered people. Just like father in the prodigal son story, God welcomed Israel back together through a man named Nehemiah. Even while His people were scattered across the world, God continued protecting them.

———

When I think about these kings and kingdoms, I am confronted with the harsh reality of the consequences of sin. God has created laws that help us understand how to love and relate to Him and how to live well with each other.

I know, process, and accept God's laws as truth; however, practicing them is a different matter. I'm a good bit like Rehoboam. I've been told what will bring happiness, longevity, and peace; but I choose the opposite instead. I rebel against God. I wage war against His kingdom. My heart wanders like Solomon's and I build places to worship idols in my mind. The result is pain, suffering, insecurity, fear, and a bitterness that takes root in my soul. My kingdom crumbles under the weight of self-importance and false worship.

The consequences of sin are both emotionally and physically real. Choices we make can corrupt and ruin our existence. We can certainly end up sitting in slop with no place to go.

I am convinced that God's design for His people is love. His plan is faithful and undeserved mercy.

At the same time that the Southern Kingdom was falling, the prophet Micah had a message from God.

"But you, O Bethlehem Ephrathah, who are too little to be among the clans of Judah, from you shall come forth for me one who is to be ruler in Israel, whose coming forth is from of old, from ancient days. Therefore he shall give them up until the time when she who is in labor has given birth; then the rest of his brothers shall return to the people of Israel. And he shall stand and shepherd his flock in the strength of the LORD, in the majesty of the name of the LORD his God. And they shall dwell secure, for now he shall be great to the ends of the earth. And he shall be their peace" (Micah 5:2–5).

A Shepherd like His ancestor David will come and bring peace to the ends of the earth. A child, the offspring of Eve, will be born in Bethlehem. He will bring peace to Israel and the world. God's plan is peace for a world that does not deserve it. This is God's design for salvation.

Reflection

Read 2 Samuel 7:4–17, 1 Kings 3:3–14, Micah 3:9–12, and Luke 15:11–32 again. Take your time. Think about what's been connected so far in God's story of redemption. Slow down; pretend this is the first time you've read these chapters. Think about the words you are reading.

1. As you think about the kings that God chose for Israel, name a few ways they highlighted God's glory through their service. Also, name specific ways power corrupted each of them.
2. Why was Solomon's betrayal of God so significant that it caused the kingdom to split?
3. The description of Israel's sin in Micah 3:9–12 is particularly troubling. What patterns of sin and separation from God did you notice as you read this part of the history of Israel?
4. Have you ever wandered from trusting God during a time of blessing in your life?
5. Take a moment and consider the consequences of sin in your life. What insecurities and fears do you face from your past choices?
6. How does God's forgiveness and protection for His people bring you encouragement?

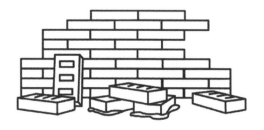

CHAPTER 7

Restoration

Israel had split in half. Solomon's leadership had allowed idol worship. Nobody even blinked. They just kept worshipping other gods; they even built places to worship these false deities. The people continued to rebel and the kings joined them. God allowed enemies to come and destroy the kingdom that was meant for greater things. Israel was in ruins.

It appeared that God's people were unsalvageable. From an outsider's standpoint, God had let His nation fall apart. It looked like God had called it a day.

The people were oppressed and scattered across the earth. They lived in foreign kingdoms that thought nothing of God or His glory. For the most part, the Jewish people were just trying to get by. (I imagine them putting "When in Persia" bumper stickers on their carts.) Local customs were creeping into the lives of each

Hebrew family. They were also making a choice about the local religion. Would they continue to follow their God?

During this time, there were great stories of the best and brightest Hebrew people being selected for leadership in other countries. Daniel, Esther, and Nehemiah all made significant impacts in their respective countries. In most situations, these Jewish men and women were forced to make a choice between their new home that had "blessed" them and the God they were holding on to from their past. In each story, we see God move to defend His people and continue to overcome false gods.

God's chosen people were left vulnerable and scattered. This again raises the question: If God had promised to make a great nation and bless the world through Abraham's family, how would He do it? Additionally, God made a promise that the reign of David would never end. How was that going to happen?

Though they didn't deserve it, God promised to bring the people of Israel back together. And it's remarkable how He did it.

Read Ezekiel 20:33–44.

While Israel was experiencing this crumbled kingdom dispersion, the prophet Ezekiel spoke the Word of the Lord. God told them that He was going to save them and bring them back together. God said, "I will be king over you" (20:33). In this prophecy, God also said that Israel would repent and make costly burnt offerings for their sins. Their repentance would be pleasing to God and He would return them to the land He promised them. But the "how" remained a mystery. It didn't sound like a Noah, Abraham, Moses, Joseph, or even a David-type leader would rise; God stated that He would be king over them. The book of Ezra solves the mystery of how.

Read Ezra 1:1–11.

Ezra says "the LORD stirred up the spirit of Cyrus king of Persia" (1:1). (Sometimes I stumble over details in the Bible. I miss the value of a sentence because I'm looking for some other answer. I've seen God's Spirit move in power throughout the Old Testament many times. Yet as I read this chapter in Ezra, I couldn't help but be wowed again.) God stirred the spirit of a pagan king. Kings think a lot of themselves. Absolute power brings out the worst forms of selfishness. Why would a pagan king want Israel to come back together? There was no financial gain to be had. Israel had been defeated. All their treasures had been taken. Restoring Israel would require money and resources to come from somewhere. It makes no sense for a pagan king to help the broken kingdom of Israel.

There are other places in the Bible where God uses pagans for His purposes. There is even a text in Habakkuk where the prophet pleads with God to stop doing so (Habakkuk 1:6–13)! But it's particularly surprising to have a king who doesn't believe in God choose to save God's people.

Israel deserved the wrath of God because they had rejected Him completely. Their abundant sin and disobedience caused the kingdom to crash and allowed their enemies to rule. God permitted a pagan king to do what he did best: destroy, conquer, and capture. It isn't strange to think about a pagan king trying to expand his kingdom or make his name great in the land. But, it is quite shocking to think about a pagan king being moved by the Spirit of God to do the opposite. God compelled a king to do something completely opposed to his nature.

The king of Persia decreed that a temple be built to the God of a captive people . . . and he paid for it himself. He gave back the treasures that were taken from Israel; he returned the wealth of a captive nation. (I guess a king can do whatever he pleases, but I wonder what his advisors thought while this was happening. I bet they thought he had lost his mind.)

God's plan and purpose cannot be stopped. This is His story and His design. God did not restore Israel because they deserved it. He didn't do it because the punishment had lasted long enough. He didn't restore Israel because they earned it. God saves, redeems, and restores for the purpose of His name. God said: "And you shall know that I am the LORD, when I deal with you for my name's sake, not according to your evil ways, nor according to your corrupt deeds, O house of Israel, declares the Lord GOD" (Ezekiel 20:44).

At that time, Jerusalem was in shambles. The city walls had been torn apart and no one was safe in the city. That's why everyone left. It wasn't just that Israel had crumbled as a nation, but the fortified walls had quite literally crumbled around it. Pagan kings were in power over Israel and God used their authority to grant Hebrew leaders permission to start rebuilding. God used His faithful people—men like Ezra and Nehemiah—to rebuild Jerusalem and the temple. God called Israel to return to the Promised Land; but some of the Hebrew people chose to stay where they were. They refused His offer. Israel needed God even though they didn't want Him.

God saved Israel because He is God. For His glory, He kept His word. Again, we see God keep His promise. I guess if God can cause an elderly couple to have a child, He can certainly give a king a surprising idea. The king of Persia waved his hand and Israel was on its way to being put back together.

A significant part of this restoration came with repentance from certain Hebrew people. Nehemiah was one of them. Nehemiah's heart was broken by all that Israel experienced. Read his prayer to God:

"Let your ear be attentive and your eyes open, to hear the prayer of your servant that I now pray before you day and night for the people of Israel your servants, confessing the sins of the people of Israel, which we have sinned against you. Even I and my father's house have sinned. We have acted very corruptly against you and have not kept the commandments, the statutes, and

the rules that you commanded your servant Moses. Remember the word that you commanded your servant Moses, saying, 'If you are unfaithful, I will scatter you among the peoples'" (Nehemiah 1:6–8).

God used Nehemiah and Ezra to lead Israel back to Jerusalem. They rebuilt the city and its walls. God was king and this restoration was for His glory. However, Israel did not govern itself any longer. God restored the nation, but it wasn't the same as before. They still lived under the rule of others.

———

The time of Israel's dispersion throughout the world is difficult to process. The Hebrew people caused such adversity for themselves. Israel acted like an abusive spouse who repeatedly breaks the vows of marriage. The fallout from their serial adultery was extensive. The consequences of sin were painful and evident.

Israel's unfaithfulness highlights God's consistent love for them. He restored them, not because they deserved it, but for His glory. God showed the world His faithfulness to Israel. That is a glorious sight to behold. The way in which God restored Israel is a tremendous reminder that He can do anything. God compelled a pagan King to not only restore Israel, but to give them the money to finance it! The Lord can use bad things, even bad people, for good and for His glory.

The story of the dispersion reminds me that nothing is beyond restoration. Israel could not do anything worse than what was already done. They had committed every sin against God. Their rebellion was exhaustive. Yet, God was committed to restoring them. God's love made a way for Israel to return to the Promised Land. Nothing is beyond redemption.

These truths apply directly to me. I do not deserve God either. In spirit and practice, I'm just like Israel. God showers His love on me and I gladly accept it. Then I go off and do what I want. My selfishness knows no bounds. I wake up, live my day, and go to sleep thinking about myself. My calendar and my bank account tell a story of idol worship. I know what God calls me to do, but often I choose my wants first.

As was true for Israel, God's love isn't about me, it is about God. God's love for me highlights His glory and goodness. God restores me even though I don't deserve it; He can restore anything. God's salvation in my life does not happen because I've earned it. It is from God alone.

Hundreds of years after Jerusalem was rebuilt, the Apostle Paul talked about how God saves us. He said, "For by grace you have been saved through faith. And this is not your own doing; it is the gift of God" (Ephesians 2:8). Paul's words make it clear that salvation comes solely through Jesus Christ. Faith in Christ alone makes us right in the eyes of God. Only God can save us, not our good works.

All of this points to the fact that nothing is beyond restoration. It doesn't matter what I've done, what I'm doing, or what might happen in my life, God can restore anything. Nothing is impossible for God. I have witnessed the miracles of His restoration. I've watch the blinders fall off of men absorbed in selfish addictions. I've seen God do the unthinkable. (I wonder if God laughs every time we are surprised by what He can do.)

How can we be more like Nehemiah? God desires repentance. Nehemiah basically said, "I'm wrong, my family is wrong, my people have been wrong. God, only You can save us." Repentant hearts renew our relationship with God. A repentant heart agrees with God about sin and desires to be forgiven and made right. 1 John 1:9 says, "If we confess our sins, he is faithful and just to forgive us our sins and to cleanse us from all unrighteousness."

If I have trusted Christ with my life, things are different. I don't deserve salvation, but I've been given it. I've been restored; again,

God has done the miraculous. I experience peace with God because of His love. The only response to such a transformation is a life given completely to Christ. My thoughts, actions, and life should point to God for His glory. I want everyone to know that God can restore anything. God can redeem anyone. He restored Israel, He redeemed me, and anyone can be saved through faith. Nothing is impossible for God. This is God's design for salvation for the world.

In the history of Israel's dispersion, I see Jesus in the way God set out to provide for Israel even when they were not together as a nation. God put people in positions of authority to redeem His people. God changed the minds of pagan kings to restore a nation that did not deserve it. These acts of God protected Abraham's family and maintained God's blessing. They also kept Israel together so David's lineage could produce a Messiah who will save the people.

Jesus will rule forever. God's plan continues to unfold even though Israel doesn't deserve it.

Reflection

Read Ezekiel 20:33–44, Ezra 1:1–11, and Nehemiah 1. Take your time. Think about what's been connected so far in God's story of redemption. Slow down. Pretend this is the first time you've read it. Think about the words you are reading.

1. Why does God bring Israel back together? What future significance could this have for God's promises to Israel?
2. How does God's forgiveness encourage Israel's commitment to Him as they return to rebuild Jerusalem?
3. How does Nehemiah repent in his prayer to God?
4. What encouragement for your life do you find in God's restoration of Israel? Are there things you have done that you consider unforgiveable? What has been done *to* you? Is it possible that God could bring healing to your life in these areas?
5. When you accept God's forgiveness for your sins, how are you encouraged to respond to what He has done for you?
6. How does repentance impact your relationship with God and others?

CHAPTER 8
Shot Called

The king of Israel was not the only powerful voice in God's kingdom. God used prophets to speak His words to His people. They existed from Judges up until the ministry of Jesus Christ.

Isaiah was a prophet in the Southern Kingdom of Israel; he lived 100 years before the Southern Kingdom fell and long before Ezra and Nehemiah helped restore the Promised Land. Honestly, he didn't have much luck with anyone responding to his messages. The people of Israel, as we have seen, were not very interested in the things of God. Isaiah lived 100 years.

Isaiah's message was a picture of Isaiah's life with God. Whether or not anyone listened, Isaiah was faithful to God. Whether or not Israel paid attention to God, the Lord had never stopped being faithful to them. Isaiah's words were meant to be encouragement in the present and clear direction for the future.

Read Isaiah 43:1–25.

Isaiah predicted that God would bring Israel back together. He would "gather" them together (Isaiah 43:5). When this gathering happened, it was for one reason; it was not because Israel deserved it, it was because Israel belonged to God. God told Israel, "You are mine" (Isaiah 43:1). (I find it interesting to consider that God's redemption for Israel had very little to do with Israel.) According to God, Israel didn't call out to Him. They didn't pray to Him. God's chosen people did not offer sacrifices for the forgiveness of their sins. They didn't do anything to deserve God's redemption, but God chose to forgive their sins and restore them for His glory. God said, "I, I am he who blots out your transgressions for my own sake, and I will not remember your sins" (Isaiah 43:25).

God forgives for His own glory. Look at how God used Isaiah to reveal a bigger piece of His design puzzle:

> *"And now the LORD says, he who formed me from the womb to be his servant, to bring Jacob back to him; and that Israel might be gathered to him— for I am honored in the eyes of the LORD, and my God has become my strength— he says: 'It is too light a thing that you should be my servant to raise up the tribes of Jacob and to bring back the preserved of Israel; I will make you as a light for the nations, that my salvation may reach to the end of the earth'" (Isaiah 49:5, 6).*

It is interesting to consider what people must have been thinking when they heard Isaiah speak. Isaiah talked about someone being formed in a womb to be a servant. His message went from reuniting Israel to God's plan to do something that would be seen across the globe: His offer of salvation to all. Beyond Israel, God had a plan for everyone. God's plan seemed to revolve around the idea of a servant, a servant who would save. But this servant-savior didn't sound like a light to the world. It sounded like he wouldn't be received well. Isaiah had dark words for this servant who would save.

Read Isaiah 52:13—53:12.

The prophet Isaiah spoke these words 700 years before the birth of Jesus. He talked about a servant who would save the world. How would He save the world? The servant would act wisely (52:13) and then be lifted high and marred beyond recognition (52:14). Ultimately, this servant would "sprinkle" many nations (52:15). In the time of the prophets, priests would sprinkle the blood of an unblemished lamb as a sacrifice for the forgiveness of sins. It was called a sin offering. Does that sound familiar? Jesus would willingly give up His life for the sins of the world. Ultimately, He would serve everyone by the sprinkling of His blood.

Isaiah told the kingdom of Judah that God would redeem them through a servant who would be known as a "man of sorrows" (53:3). He would carry the sorrows of the world. As a punishment for the sins that God's people committed, this servant would be pierced. The servant would be crushed for their inequities and the world would be healed through His wounds (53:5).

God's promise from Genesis 3:15 should not be forgotten. Isaiah's message reminds us that God said He would "put enmity between [the serpent] and the woman," and ultimately, her offspring would crush the head of the serpent.

It is fascinating to think about what the people must have been processing as they were listening to Isaiah. Israel wasn't really listening to God, much less Isaiah. The Lord was not telling them what would happen so they'd know; He was telling the world for the purpose of His glory. God was calling His shot.

I grew up playing baseball. I loved everything about the game. I loved the smell of the leather glove, my uniform, and having permission to slide in the dirt. Anyone who plays baseball loves to imagine what it would be like to hit a homerun. Actually hitting a home run is even better than imagining it. But what if you predicted it beforehand?

The 1932 World Series is the stuff of legend. Babe Ruth walked up to bat and pointed his bat out to centerfield. The next moment, Ruth hit a homerun . . . right to centerfield! It sounds too good to be true, but it was recorded on film in 1932[2]. He called his shot.

Every child declares, at some point, that they will become the President of the United States of America. Only a rare few ever make good on that promise. Many other children hope to be astronauts and walk on the moon. The list of people who fulfill those promises is very short. People make big promises all the time, but follow-through is hard to come by.

God used Isaiah to speak His words to His people around 700BC[3]. God told everyone that He was going to send a servant who would be exalted and crushed. He would be pierced and crushed for the sins of the people. The death of this servant would satisfy God and make many people righteous (Isaiah 53:11). 700 years before it happened, God called His shot!

Isaiah was not the only prophet God used to call His shot. Jeremiah, Daniel, Zechariah, Malachi, and Micah (just to name a few) all proclaimed a message of good news about this servant to come. Then, there were 400 years of silence between the time of the prophets and the coming of Jesus. God did not speak one word of hope, redemption, or mercy for four centuries . . . nothing.

Not speaking for 400 years doesn't really sound like something God would do, but God had a reason for the silence. Knowing the big picture of God's story can be helpful because God had done this before.

In Genesis, God gave Abram a dream and told him that he would birth a great nation. But He also promised hardship to Abram's family. God told Abram to "know for certain that your offspring will be sojourners in a land that is not theirs and will be servants there, and they will be afflicted for four hundred years" (Genesis 15:13). This prediction came true. For 400 years, Israel suffered as slaves in Egypt. Just as God promised, He revealed Himself to a man named Moses. The Lord told Moses, "I have surely seen the affliction of my people who are in Egypt and have heard their cry because of their taskmasters. I know their sufferings, and I have come down to deliver them out of the hand of the Egyptians" (Exodus 3:7, 8). None of this was an accident.

In God's perfect design, He had been preparing the world for salvation since the beginning of creation.

God's first response after the fall of mankind was hope. He declared that sin would be defeated. The head of the serpent would be crushed.

When sin ran wild on the earth, God chose one man, Noah, to save humanity. Because Noah wasn't perfect, sin continued to cause the hearts of humanity to wander.

God selected a nobody from nowhere named Abram to bless the world. Abram was an old man, married to an old woman with no possibility for children. Abraham became a father to Isaac when he was 100-years-old. From Isaac, the nation of Israel was formed. This nation was supposed to be an example to the world of God's goodness. God protected and provided for Israel, but they chose selfishness and sin at every opportunity.

God set Israel up to be a kingdom of priests, but all Israel wanted was a king. God still used His people to show the world His glory.

As Israel continually sinned against God, the Kingdom fell and the people were scattered. God saved them through pagan kings and foreign rulers. God restored and forgave Israel, not because they earned it, but because He was filled with mercy.

All of this was completed by design. God kept His promises. It was God's plan all along to redeem and bless the whole world through His servant. 700 years before Jesus, Isaiah talked about Him. 300 years after Isaiah, God fell silent. There was not a word for 400 years.

———

There have been times in my life when it seemed that God was silent. It felt like God had nothing to say to me. I would ask, pray, and even beg to hear from God.

When I study God's Word, I am reminded how much I am like Israel. Israel was far from perfect. They messed up just about every chance they got. That sounds a lot like me. Yet there were also times when Israel begged for God's mercy. They wept over their sin and asked God to forgive them and be with them. There were times that Israel longed for God's presence. I can relate to that.

Two different times, Israel waited 400 years to hear from God and I don't like to wait for anything. This is especially true when I think I need direction from God. I have felt alone. I've felt God's silence in my life. I'm not saying it was actually real, but it felt like it was. Maybe you've felt this way also. When I go through dark seasons and I feel far from God, I am reminded of a few important truths: we must trust what God has done; and we must trust in His promises. We must be honest with ourselves and trust God enough that we are enabled to take steps of faith.

We must trust what God has done. Growing in knowledge of the Bible helps us to understand God's timing. Every story is a building block that tells of God's supreme faithfulness. Remember Isaiah's prophecy: the promise of a servant. This servant was to be born of a woman. We know Isaiah's servant is to be the savior of the world. God promised a servant whose soul would be poured out for the transgressions of the world (Isaiah 53:12). God kept this promise. This gives me hope when I feel alone. God's design proves to me that we can trust Him. He has never failed to keep a promise. He has always been faithful. God's plans are good and we can trust Him.

We must trust God's promises. I think about the promises that God made in Isaiah and how God faithfully made them happen with Jesus. Knowing this helps me to remember that God follows through on His promises. I must not forget this, especially when I feel alone. God's Word helps me know that I am not on my own. God has promised His presence in the lives of His followers. God is with us.

I also believe I should be honest about my sin.

Nehemiah poured out his soul to God. He asked for forgiveness for his specific sins, the sins of his family, and the sins of Israel (Nehemiah 1:6–8). He wasn't playing around. Nehemiah knew the ways he had sinned against God. He and his family had false idols in their hearts.

A few thousand years later, nothing has changed. I must be honest with myself about my ego, neediness, and selfish thinking. My sinful nature affects how I hear God and follow Him.

You need to be honest about your sin, too. Selfishness can destroy your life. You must be honest about your idols, your self-promoting ways, and the sin that drags you down. You have to be transparent about sin's effect on your relationship with God.

Lastly, we must trust God to take steps of faith. If we remember what God has done, God is never silent in our lives. He speaks to us through His past faithfulness. Trusting what God has done in the past helps us to see Him in the present. We must consider ourselves new creations in God's eyes and try to live for Him— in response to what He has done through Jesus Christ. If we believe in Christ, then we must live for Christ in every moment.

This means that I have to forgive people who have hurt me; I must forgive them because I know how God has forgiven me. I must sacrificially love others because I have been loved. My life should be an example of what God has done.

You are also called to forgive. You must forgive because Christ has forgiven you. This is a form of sacrificial love to others. What you do should reflect Christ because of everything Jesus has done for you.

You can't miss Jesus in the time of prophets because they specifically predict His coming. Isaiah was outrageously specific, and it doesn't stop with him. The prophet Micah practically gives GPS coordinates to the birthplace of the Messiah. He says, "But you, O Bethlehem Ephrathah, who are too little to be among the clans of Judah, from you shall come forth for me one who is to be ruler in Israel, whose coming forth is from of old, from ancient days" (Micah 5:2).

After 400 years of silence, one last prophet appeared. The account of Jesus' life begins with a quote from Isaiah and the introduction of a man named John.

Read Mark 1:1–8.

Isaiah not only predicted the life of Jesus, but also the life of a prophet known as John the Baptist.

John the Baptist preached a message of repentance, claiming God's Kingdom was near. It wasn't thousands of years away, or even 400 years away. God's Kingdom was arriving as John spoke. God would soon bring about His promise of a servant, Messiah, and Savior.

Reflection

Read Isaiah 43:1–28, 52:13—53:12, and Mark 1:1–8 again. Take your time. Think about what's been connected so far in God's story of redemption. Slow down; pretend this is the first time you've read this. Think about the words you are reading.

1. In Isaiah 43, what are the reasons God brings His people back together?
2. Write down all the predictions about Jesus you find in Isaiah 52:13—53:12.
3. How do you see God's plan for redemption coming together in these Old Testament stories?
4. How does knowing God's plan to send Jesus help you with your struggles?
5. When you think about what God has done in your past, how does it strengthen your faith?
6. How can your understanding of God's Word help you take small steps of faith?

CHAPTER 9

Jesus

John the Baptist said, "After me comes he who is mightier than I, the strap of whose sandals I am not worthy to stoop down and untie. I have baptized you with water, but he will baptize you with the Holy Spirit" (Mark 1:7, 8).

The best way to describe John the Baptist is as *a throwback*. He looked and sounded like he was from ancient days. His persona was startling, but may have been exactly what some people hoped for. After 400 years of a silence, a prophet from God spoke again. John the Baptist shouted on the outskirts of town, "Repent, be baptized! The Kingdom of God is near!" (Mark 1:4). This was the beginning of what God had promised for thousands of years.

If you've ever picked up the Bible and started reading the New Testament, the beginning probably seems like a strange way to start. The first book is *Matthew*. The first chapter reads like a list of the things you should never name a child. ("Jehoshaphat" [Matthew 1:8] would be a tough name to recover from in middle school.) All these strange names make up a specific lineage.

Read Matthew 1.

The very first verse of Matthew explains why this "list" is so important. "The book of the genealogy of Jesus Christ, the son of David, the son of Abraham" (Matthew 1:1). Chapter 1 is an explanation of how God kept His promises to Abraham and David. Jesus is the answer to Abraham's blessing and David's family's eternal reign.

God's plan for keeping His promise was filled with colorful choices—the people in the lineage of Jesus Christ.

Usually, a genealogy would name the men of the lineage. This genealogy has references to five women. Each one has an amazing story. Tamar dressed up like a prostitute to seduce her father-in-law, but was still called "righteous" (Genesis 38). Rahab was an actual prostitute and a traitor, but became a part of the family of God (Joshua 2). Ruth was a non-Jewish widow who trusted God because of her love for her mother-in-law (Ruth 1:4). Bathsheba had an adulterous relationship with King David, but ushered in the golden age of Israel (2 Samuel 11:4). And Mary was a virgin who birthed God's Son (Matthew 1:23). (It is impossible to sum up these stories with just a few words. You should go read them.) Each story is a rich account of the different ways God saves, restores, and responds to His people.

The lineage of Jesus displays God's power. Through Israel's creation, exodus from Egypt, journey to the Promised Land, the development of their kingdom and its destruction, God kept His promises to Abraham and David. All along, the plan was Jesus. All of God's blessing is fulfilled in Jesus Christ.

This is further proof that God can do anything: He sent His Son to be the Savior of the world. Instead of a man with military might, God came near in the form of a baby. The Savior was born in a little town with the most unexpected witnesses.

Read Luke 2:1–21.

A baby was born in a stable in the little town of Bethlehem. This baby was named Jesus. The Savior of the world was revealed to a small group of shepherds on the side of a hill; they were visited by a glorious host of angels. After they heard the news, they ran into town looking for a baby in a manger (Luke 2:12). I think it is safe to assume that this was not the majestic Messiah everyone expected. However, this was exactly the Messiah God had predicted throughout history.

Baby Jesus grew up. He had parents and a fairly normal life. The Bible doesn't spend a lot of time on His upbringing. It simply says that "Jesus increased in wisdom and in stature and in favor with God and man" (Luke 2:52).

I am sure some people were talking about everything John the Baptist was saying. They hoped for a Messiah to come. A foreign government still oppressed Israel. Life was difficult and they were ready to be saved. They probably talked about a miraculous salvation like what happened in Egypt with Moses. Maybe they hoped God would come and destroy their Roman oppressors! Moses had shown up with signs and wonders; was it possible the coming Messiah would overthrow Rome in the same way?

Jesus began His ministry by being baptized by John the Baptist. John declared, "Behold, the Lamb of God, who takes away the sin of the world!" (John 1:29). God spoke from the heavens saying, "You are my beloved Son; with you I am well pleased" (Luke 3:22). From this moment, Jesus began recruiting disciples and teaching whomever would listen. Jesus performed miracles. Jesus taught in ways that people had never heard before. Jesus drew a crowd.

One of the men who found himself fascinated with Jesus was Nicodemus.

Read John 3:1–21.

Born again. Today, if you were to hear someone say that they were "born again," you wouldn't think much of it. It's a common phrase; but back then, not so much. When Nicodemus heard it for the first time, he thought about warning his mom. This conversation was pointing to the way Jesus would bless the world. This moment was foretelling the salvation Jesus would bring for Israel and everyone else. Jesus wouldn't overtake Rome with force. He wouldn't become an earthly ruler at all. Jesus was talking about *spiritual* rebirth. He told Nicodemus to look beyond physical things to a spiritual salvation.

Jesus summed up the Good News by saying, "For God so loved the world, that he gave his only Son, that whoever believes in him should not perish but have eternal life. For God did not send his Son into the world to condemn the world, but in order that the world might be saved through him" (John 3:16, 17). Jesus told Nicodemus that the way to eternal life was spiritual rebirth through faith in the Son of God. This was the unveiling of God's design to save not only Israel, but the entire world.

We don't know what Nicodemus thought. He came in darkness of night to determine whether Jesus was the promised Messiah. He was convinced that Jesus had God's power, but he wanted to know if Jesus was the One. Jesus told Nicodemus that the way to eternal life was belief in the Son of God. This was an accepted phrase in the Jewish faith. Many times in the Bible, the Messiah was described as the Son of Man or the Son of God. Nicodemus had heard of the Son of God. He knew that meant "messiah." He got an answer to his question, but could he believe Jesus?

Nicodemus was a Jewish leader. He knew God's Law as well as anyone. What Jesus said was radical. Jesus essentially said that people could be made right with God if they believed in His Son. Nicodemus knew that a sacrifice was required according to God's Law (Leviticus 5:10). Jesus seemed to be saying something new, but Nicodemus didn't know what Jesus knew. He didn't know God's plan. God had prepared the ultimate sin sacrifice before creation even happened.

Read Luke 22:63—23:56.

I have been a Christian for a long time, but I still choke up reading the story of the cross. I don't like thinking about the ways Jesus was beaten. It seems painfully unfair. Jesus did nothing wrong and was punished with criminals. He was humiliated. Jesus was stripped naked and nailed to a cross meant for murderers. Jesus experienced suffocation and death. It didn't look like a glorious moment of God's victory with the coming of a Messiah. It looked like a tragedy.

Jesus knew what God had designed. He was there before the creation of the world. He was present at the fall of mankind. From the offspring of Eve came Jesus. God's redemption came in the form of a completely innocent man—a man free from sin—giving up His life as a sacrifice for the sins of the world. This was God's blessing and salvation.

Peter, one of Jesus' disciples, summed up what Christ did on the cross like this: "For Christ also suffered once for sins, the righteous for the unrighteous, that he might bring us to God, being put to death in the flesh but made alive in the spirit" (1 Peter 3:18). This was a one-time sacrifice for all of the people of the world. God brought blessing and forgiveness to anyone who would believe—spiritual rebirth.

We don't know what happened with Nicodemus. John 19:38–42 tells us he showed up at the tomb. It is impossible to know whether

Nicodemus made the connection that an innocent man giving up His life fulfilled the required sin offering. But he was a student of Scripture. Nicodemus knew that sin separated the world from God. Because of sin, mankind earned death. The only thing that brought forgiveness to God's people was a sacrificial offering. It was John the Baptist who had called Jesus "The Lamb of God" (John 1:29). I wonder if Nicodemus thought about the meaning of this death while he prepared the body of the Christ. He certainly could not have known what was coming next.

Read Matthew 28:1–10.

Through the life, death, and resurrection of Jesus Christ, God defeated sin and death. He overcame the constant failures of Israel. God chose Israel so the world would see His greatness. God's glory was fully on display in Jesus Christ. This was God's design of salvation for those who believe. It had always been His plan, and Jesus knew it well.

Read Luke 24:13–27.

Jesus didn't just explain the details of the previous few days to those two travelers on the road. He explained everything, all the way back to Moses, the Ten Commandments, and all the prophets. Jesus explained to them how He was the Messiah. Those travelers got to hear Jesus explain God's plan of salvation throughout history. God's plan was never changed or revised. Prophecy after prophecy, over thousands of years, pointed to specific moments in Jesus' life . . . even the way He would die.

God's plan was to have a reverse Noah. Rather than one man being saved while the whole world was destroyed, Jesus gave up His life so the entire world could be saved. Jesus was a more perfect Moses. Moses tried to give up his life for Israel. He asked God to be blotted "out of your book you have written" (Exodus 32:32). God reminded Moses that only a perfect person could answer for God's people. Jesus was the perfect One. He gave up His life for people who didn't deserve it.

No one could have known it would work this way, but this was exactly how God had intended to bless the world through Abraham (Genesis 12:3). Though King David was a man after God's own heart, he was far from perfect. Jesus was the fulfillment of God's never-ending reign. John the Baptist was not worthy to tie His sandals. Jesus was completely perfect in every way. His death and resurrection was a perfect plan by God's design.

———

It is impossible for me to read Scripture without comparing it to my life. I am Israel. We are Israel. I'm not talking about our lineage. We are Israel in the way that we treat the Lord. God has revealed Himself to us. We know of His truth and the beauty of His creation. You and I know how we should relate to God and to the world. We know we are supposed to love God and others, but we don't do it.

Over and over, I practice selfish sinfulness at every turn, just like Israel. I practice idol worship with my things, my money, and my time. I have built a world of me; for this, I deserve death. We all do. Our kingdoms deserve to be crumbled. We deserve to be separated from God.

But here's the most amazing truth: God loves us. He doesn't love us for what we have or haven't done. God doesn't love us because we have followed His rules more perfectly than others. He just loves us. God loves us because we belong to Him. We have seen His perfect love through what He has done on the cross. We know God loves us because of Jesus.

Salvation is by design. Just like Nicodemus, you must consider the reality of being born again. God reveals His plan for salvation through the cross of Jesus. You can respond to what Christ has done through faith. While you cannot be good enough to be saved, you also can't be bad enough to be disqualified. The only way to salvation in Christ is through faith. You must believe what Jesus has done and that He alone offers salvation.

Belief in Jesus Christ brought salvation to my life. I came to faith in Jesus when I was nine years old. I knelt on the green shag carpet in my parent's bedroom and prayed with my mom. I was born again. A few weeks later, I met with my pastor and parents and I felt led to follow Christ in baptism. I wanted everyone to know what Christ had done in my life!

Have you been born again? I'd like for you to take a moment and prayerfully think about everything you have read about God and His plan for the world. Consider God's design for salvation. Do you believe Jesus is the Son of God? Have you given your faith and trust to Christ? Maybe this moment is a chance for you to give your life to Him. All you have to do is pray to God and tell Him that you believe Jesus is Lord. Ask God to forgive you and make you right in His eyes. God's design for salvation through Jesus is for you today—right now.

What happens next in the Bible is pretty amazing; we get to witness the Acts of the Apostles. More specifically, we will see the power of God's Holy Spirit on display in every believer's life. The early Christians who began to tell the world about Jesus didn't do it alone. (Acts answers some questions about our lives also.)

The birth of the church is up next.

Reflection

Read John 3:1–21 and Luke 24:13–27 again. Take your time. Think about what's been connected so far in God's story of redemption. Slow down; pretend this is the first time you've read this. Think about the words you are reading.

1. After reading Luke 24:13–27, write down the ways you remember God fulfilling His promises from the Old Testament through Jesus Christ.
2. In John 3:1–21, Nicodemus hears the idea of being "born again" for the first time. How would you describe this spiritual process to someone who wasn't a Christian?
3. When you consider Jesus' life, death, and resurrection, how do you see God's love for you?
4. Are you a Christian? Think about your life. When have you responded to the Good News of Jesus and how are you different?
5. How does understanding more about God's Word help you to place your faith in Jesus?
6. In what ways does knowing God's plan compel you to live for Him today?

CHAPTER 10

The Holy Spirit

Jesus came back from the dead. God overcame the impossible, and death was defeated. Jesus' followers watched as He was buried and sealed into a tomb. Three days later, He dropped by to say "hello." 1 Corinthians 15 tells of those who witnessed the resurrection of Jesus.

". . . Christ died for our sins in accordance with the Scriptures, that he was buried, that he was raised on the third day in accordance with the Scriptures, and that he appeared to Cephas, then to the twelve. Then he appeared to more than five hundred brothers at one time . . ." (1 Corinthians 15:3–6).

Our culture is pretty good at fooling us. Computer generated images cause us to question reality. Video footage is manipulated. Fake news is as prevalent as real news. Sometimes it is hard to know what to believe. The disciples faced a similar issue. They didn't know what to think. Jesus was standing before them, scars on His body, alive and in the flesh.

Jesus remained on Earth for forty days after the resurrection (Acts 1:3). During this time, Jesus spent time with His people. He encouraged their faith and even shared a few meals with them! (See Luke 24:42 and John 21:12.) Nonetheless, it was hard to believe.

One of my favorite moments comes from a disciple named Thomas. He wouldn't believe anything until he put his finger in the wounds of his crucified master. Jesus told Thomas, "Put your finger here, and see my hands; and put out your hand, and place it in my side. Do not disbelieve, but believe" (John 20:27).

After each appearance of the resurrected Christ, the disciples must have wondered what would come next. It didn't seem like Rome was going to be toppled. It felt like something bigger than that. The entire world had been transformed. What would come next? After appearances, meals, and scars, Jesus had a purpose for their future.

"Now the eleven disciples went to Galilee, to the mountain to which Jesus had directed them. And when they saw him they worshiped him, but some doubted. And Jesus came and said to them, "All authority in heaven and on earth has been given to me. Go therefore and make disciples of all nations, baptizing them in the name of the Father and of the Son and of the Holy Spirit, teaching them to observe all that I have commanded you. And behold, I am with you always, to the end of the age" (Matthew 28:16–20).

I wish I could say where I would have landed on the belief spectrum had I lived during those days. It seems both surprising and obvious that some of Jesus' followers doubted. How could they not? Jesus was crucified in front of them; days later, He was leading them on a hike up a mountain! It was hard to believe. But, they had seen Jesus walk on water. Jesus had healed the lame and blind. He even raised a man from the dead. And the disciples witnessed it all. This had to mess with their minds. There really could be only two responses: worship or doubt.

On top of the mountain just before He rose to heaven, Jesus brought clarity and purpose to the disciples' lives. He gave them something to accomplish: An unending mission that we are still called to live out today. Matthew 28:18–20 is called the Great Commission. This is a call to arms from Jesus. He wants His followers to be sent out to the world. Jesus wanted His followers to spend their lives telling others the Good News about Him. The unheard-of part of this challenge came with two words: "all nations" (Matthew 28:19). That's a pretty tall order. Jesus' plan involved using fisherman from Galilee to spread His Gospel across the world. They were going to need help. The disciples began to search for clarity. They asked Jesus this question:

"So when they had come together, they asked him, 'Lord, will you at this time restore the kingdom to Israel?' He said to them, 'It is not for you to know times or seasons that the Father has fixed by his own authority. But you will receive power when the Holy Spirit has come upon you, and you will be my witnesses in Jerusalem and in all Judea and Samaria, and to the end of the earth.' And when he had said these things, as they were looking on, he was lifted up, and a cloud took him out of their sight" (Acts 1:6–9).

Jesus' answer was followed by His ascension.

Forty days passed between Jesus ascending to heaven and the arrival of the Holy Spirit. Many of Jesus' followers came together and waited. I'm sure they prayed together. They probably talked about all the things they had seen and wondered what was going to happen next. I wonder if they discussed the power Jesus told them about; it had to be on their minds. I'm sure many were fearful of the uncertain future and felt they needed God's strength. Some of them probably knew this passage from the prophet Joel in the Old Testament:

"And it shall come to pass afterward, that I will pour out my Spirit on all flesh; your sons and your daughters shall prophesy, your old men shall dream dreams, and your young men shall see visions. Even on the male and female

servants in those days I will pour out my Spirit. 'And I will show wonders in the heavens and on the earth, blood and fire and columns of smoke. The sun shall be turned to darkness, and the moon to blood, before the great and awesome day of the LORD comes. And it shall come to pass that everyone who calls on the name of the LORD shall be saved. For in Mount Zion and in Jerusalem there shall be those who escape, as the LORD has said, and among the survivors shall be those whom the LORD calls'" (Joel 2:28–32).

Waiting. Praying and waiting. Talking, praying, and waiting. I'm sure there was also a lot of hoping. There had to be uncertainty. I can easily imagine more than a few of Jesus' followers being afraid of what was coming next. If it had been me, I think every one of my insecurities would have flared up. I'm sure I would have been thinking about how I freeze up when people ask me hard questions. I'd have been praying that there would be no need to be too confrontational. I would have been concerned I would let my friends down. Many of these things had to be running through their minds. No matter how much they prepared, I don't think any one of them were ready for how God showed up next.

Read Acts 2:1–13.

When the big moment came, all the followers were together in one place. Three distinct things occurred: a sound, tongues of fire, and the ability to speak in other languages. Initially, this seems like an odd combination of events. However, as with all things Scripture, God was profoundly intentional with each detail. The church was given authority in that moment.

The first thing that happened was the sound. They heard "a sound like a mighty rushing wind, and it filled the entire house where they were sitting" (Acts 2:2). Multiple times in the Old Testament, the words "wind" and "Spirit" mean the same thing (1 Kings 19:11; Isaiah 66:15; Ezekiel 37:9–14)[4]. It is symbolic for the arrival of the presence of God. (I imagine hearing a freight train outside my window.)

Then they saw lapping flames above each person present. It is fascinating to think about how this may have looked. They were called "tongues of flames" (Acts 2:3). (I've never considered them to have looked like *fire tongues*, but it is possible.) This was a visual representation of mouths being used for God's glory. The Great Commission is a calling to go *tell* the world. Why not a visual representation of a tongue on fire? They were about to speak to the world about Jesus. Previously, when God had revealed Himself, He had used fire. Moses saw a bush that was burning (Exodus 3:2). The people of Israel followed a pillar of fire by night (Exodus 13:21). This was a huge visual image: God's fire being separated into tongues.

Finally, after the sound of wind and the image of separating fire, they began speaking in tongues. That's another way of saying they were given the ability to speak in foreign languages they didn't know. This sounds like an odd miracle. Why, out of all the possibilities, would God give them this ability? Why languages and not something cooler like walking on water? Because God was about to put together a puzzle He had been working on for thousands of years.

Pentecost was a festival during which "there were dwelling in Jerusalem Jews, devout men from every nation under heaven" (Acts 2:5). Jewish people had come together from all over the globe to worship God; but they had yet to hear the Good News of God's fulfilled promise in Jesus Christ.

Throughout this book, we have been talking about God's plan to "bless the world" through Israel (Genesis 12:3). However, at every turn, it has seemed Israel wanted nothing to do with God's design. Sometimes, it seemed God's plan was a failure.

God told Noah's descendants to multiply and spread out to take over the Earth for the purpose of making God's name great. Instead, they chose to try to make their own names great (Genesis

11:4). So God spread them out all over the Earth. It seemed like God's plan was failing.

Israel wanted a king. God allowed them one; but eventually the kings rejected God and led Israel to practice false worship. They built altars to other gods. Israel's kingdom split into two kingdoms and eventually crumbled altogether. Other nations pillaged and plundered God's chosen people. Israel was scattered across the earth. While it seemed God's plan was failing, this couldn't have been further from the truth.

By God's design, His chosen people ended up all over the globe. There were still those who believed and worshipped Him alone. These faithful Jews would return to Jerusalem during festival seasons. Pentecost brought people from all over the world who spoke different languages. It was no coincidence that the Holy Spirit's first act of empowerment resulted in Christians speaking the Good News about Jesus in everyone's native language.

The foreign Israelites went back home after Pentecost and told about Jesus. Israel's past scattering was no accident. God's plans didn't fail. In the end, God *did* show the world His love through Israel, whether they realized it or not.

When I imagine how this scene must looked, I think about twelve disciples, maybe Mary and Martha, and a few other folks being there for this big moment. They were all gathered together praying. Maybe they were getting their praise on. Most likely, they were on their knees with hands lifted high. My mind has them doing impromptu testimonies about things Jesus said to them. Then . . . BOOM! Rushing wind, fire, and a *Holy Ghost party*!

In actuality, there were 120 people present (Acts 1:15; 2:1) with 120 individual tongues of fire. 120 people walking around the crowds of Pentecost, speaking in foreign languages they had not previously known. I've never tried to count the names of Jesus' followers, but I can't name 120 individual people who followed Jesus. It's hard to even name all twelve of the disciples. When the Holy Spirit arrived, it wasn't just for the all-stars; it was for all who believed in Jesus Christ. It didn't matter where they came from or what they knew. It didn't matter whether they were men or women. It didn't matter what jobs they had before. They weren't judged by their wealth. The only thing that mattered was their faith in Jesus Christ. All who believed were given the Holy Spirit (Acts 2:4). Not just Peter, James, or John; all were equally given the Holy Spirit to show the world what God had done. They were called Christians.

These men and women were each very different. There were probably a few who were introverted. Maybe some had a fear of public speaking. Most of them were ill-equipped before God's gift of the Holy Spirit. When God fulfilled His promise from Joel 2:28–32, God's people of all sorts were empowered for making disciples all over the world.

In less than one day, thousands of people came to follow Jesus Christ. The Good News about the Christ spread like wildfire (individual tongues of fire, to be precise). Those mouths were empowered by God for His purpose of saving the world. The church took off, and it continues to grow and spread to this day. The whole world was blessed from the family of Abraham. God keeps His promises.

God brought the followers of Jesus together to continue to show the world His design. Acts 2 gives us a picture of how life looked for the Church.

"And they devoted themselves to the apostles' teaching and the fellowship, to the breaking of bread and the prayers. And awe came upon every soul, and many wonders and signs were being done through the apostles. And all who believed were together and had all things in common. And they were selling their possessions and belongings and distributing the proceeds to all, as any had need. And day by day, attending the temple together and breaking bread in their homes, they received their food with glad and generous hearts, praising

God and having favor with all the people. And the Lord added to their number day by day those who were being saved" (Acts 2:42–47).

The Bible tells us that early Christians faced persecution. Following Jesus wasn't easy. In most cases, believers were abandoned by their families. Knowing this, I still find myself in awe of how the early church operated. It didn't matter if they were rich or poor; everyone came together and took care of each other. Christians met each other's needs. Life was worship; the outside world saw a difference in how they lived. I love the part where Acts says the Christians had "favor with all the people" (Acts 2:46). The early church was empowered by God to do good. The world saw it and "the Lord added to their number day by day those who were being saved" (Acts 2:47).

———

I've always read the book of Acts and wished I could see what happened up close. The Holy Spirit arrived, the Church was born, and explosive growth took place. I'm amazed by the bravery of the early Christians. They abandoned everything for Jesus. This is where the Bible points out an extremely important detail. If you look closely at the end of Acts 2, it says that "the Lord added to their number" (Acts 2:47). You'll find the same wording in Acts 4, 10, 11, twice in 13, and also chapter 19. It's all over the place. It's not just about what the people were doing; it's about how God moved in power through them. God did (and does) the saving. God added to their number. God performed (and still performs) miracles for His glory. Throughout the book of Acts, God's power through the Holy Spirit is on display. We are also empowered for good works so we can share the Good News about Jesus. This was God's plan from the beginning.

As Christians, God has placed the Holy Spirit in our lives. God is within all who believe in Jesus Christ as Lord. This means that if we claim Christ, God has empowered us for the purpose of making disciples wherever we are. We are not alone, and we are not called to do something we can't. You and I are given encouragement and power from the Lord for His glory. It is God who moves in power. We are simply called to be faithful and live for Him. The mission has not changed since the book of Acts was lived and written—we are called to make disciples and be witnesses.

Reflection

Read Acts chapters 1 and 2 again. Take your time. Think about what's been connected so far in God's story of redemption. Slow down; pretend this is the first time you've read this. Think about the words you are reading.

1. Acts 1:8 tells Jesus' disciples that they will be His witnesses. Take a moment and think about what this really means. In what ways could the disciples be expert witnesses for Jesus?
2. Imagine if you were present in Acts 2:1–5. What words would you use to describe what that moment was like?
3. Think back through the previous nine chapters of this book. Think of God's great story of Jesus. When has it looked like God's plan wasn't working? How do we later see evidence of His perfect plan succeeding?
4. How does the empowering of the Holy Spirit give you strength and courage to share the Good News of Jesus?
5. Can you name a few ways you are different because of the Holy Spirit?
6. How are you fulfilling God's call to make disciples today?

CHAPTER 11

Now

Have you ever thought about how long it has been since Jesus ascended into heaven? It's been a really long time. I think we often have trouble considering how our lives connect with God's plan. Sometimes, it seems today and back then have very little to do with each other. About two thousand years have passed since the book of Acts. What does Jesus want from us right now?

Jesus basically floated off and disappeared; the disciples were left behind. I am sure the disciples stood there in shock with mixed emotions. They had been given some instructions, but more than likely, they were a bit confused.

In the forty days before the Holy Spirit arrived, I am sure they had lots of questions. I bet they spent some time going over every word they remembered from Jesus— especially the things He said about the future. Jesus had given them encouragement for the time between when He left and when He'd return. Jesus said this:

"Let not your hearts be troubled. Believe in God; believe also in me. In my Father's house are many rooms. If it were not so, would I have told you that I go to prepare a place for you? And if I go and prepare a place for you, I will come again and will take you to myself, that where I am you may be also"
(John 14:1–3).

Jesus will come back. God's plan for the world is for Jesus to return and take all who have placed their faith in Christ to heaven. As they faced persecution, this had to be extremely hopeful for the early Christian Church. Combining this understanding with the Great Commission brought a sense of urgency to their lives.

In Acts, you can feel the urgency. There was even a time when leaders of the early church had to deal with Christians who decided to give up on daily life. They stopped working, gave away their possessions, and simply waited because they knew Jesus was coming back soon (2 Thessalonians 3:6–15). They thought, "Who needs a job, house, or daily work when we are about to float up to heaven just like Jesus?" Some in the early church thought Jesus would be back at any moment. The Apostle Paul warned the early believers about the specifics of Jesus' return. He told them, "For you yourselves are fully aware that the day of the Lord will come like a thief in the night" (1 Thessalonians 5:2). No one knows when Jesus will return.

The early Church expected Jesus to come back at any second; but I sometimes feel we have grown complacent today. While we've given our lives to Christ and been "born again," we don't feel the urgency. We find ourselves being pulled and distracted by a selfish world.

The urgency of faithful living diminishes when you think about how many years it's been since Jesus walked the Earth. How many more years might pass before Jesus comes back? It is easy to be enticed to build your life around yourself.

I think this is one of the reasons we have gotten to the place we have in Christianity. Most of the people who claim Christ know very little about Jesus or the Bible. Some may only know what they are told when they attend worship services. The Bible has become an intimidating mountain of knowledge. It can be hard to know where to start. Stories of Noah, Abraham, Moses, and King David may have been learned as a child, but are never looked at again. As a child, we only heard parts of the story. (The dirty details of murder, adultery, and deception don't go over too well right before snack time.) As adults, we don't know all the details and we often don't bother looking for them.

Somewhere along the line, you and I may decide that we've got all the time in the world to be faithful to God. We may figure we'll try to live for God and attempt to understand His Word one day in the future; but right now, we just may decide to do the things we want to do instead. We've got time, right? It's not like Jesus is coming back today.

The problem is that we don't think Jesus will come back in our lifetimes. The New Testament believers needed to reengage with life and not just wait for Jesus to come back. They needed to be witnesses and make disciples for Christ. We need to be reminded that Jesus could come back at any moment; we need to reengage with Him. We need to be living every day like it will be the day Christ returns. Remember 1 Thessalonians 5:2? Jesus will be "like a thief in the night." He could return at any moment.

Our purpose today is the same as the early believers'. Jesus has called those who believe in Him to engage their worlds and point people to Christ. We are called to help others see how Christ has changed us and brought eternal life. Because of what God has done in Jesus, we want the world to know. God calls us to do this together.

The disciple Peter helps us make a current connection to Moses and Israel. Peter compares the followers of Jesus to God's plan for Israel. Peter said, "But you are a chosen race, a royal priesthood, a holy nation, a people for his own possession, that you may proclaim the excellencies of him who called you out of darkness into his marvelous light" (1 Peter 2:9). This sounds just like Exodus 19:6.

While most nations during Old Testament times had a king, God wanted Israel to be different. He wanted them to be a kingdom of priests. God wanted His people to be intent on serving Him in unity. The entire nation was set apart for the world to see.

God described a relationship between Himself and Israel that would help the world to see His glory. Israel failed at every turn. God however, was completely faithful and showed His glory to the world.

We now know His plan of Jesus Christ. We have seen the power of the Holy Spirit that lives within every believer. God's design has been fully revealed. Through the Holy Spirit we are able to be a kingdom of priests. We are living, breathing examples of Jesus to everyone we meet. Our opportunities to bring glory to God are right now. God called Israel a kingdom of priests (Exodus 19:6). Here in the New Testament, Peter refers to Christians as a "royal priesthood" (1 Peter 2:9). You and I aren't alone and we have been empowered by the Holy Spirit for good works.

Read 1 Corinthians 12:4–11.

Faith in Christ brings the Holy Spirit into our lives. We are supernaturally gifted and equipped for different types of service in this royal priesthood. This passage points out that there are different kinds of gifts, but they are all equal in God's eyes. Spiritual gifts are meant to be used together for God's kingdom.

To the best of my understanding, this list is not exhaustive. Paul only describes a few abilities God gives Christians. There are gifts related to speech, miracles, prophecy, and tongues to name a few. The point of this list is not to exalt one gift over any of the others. You are not more special if God has blessed you with any one of these gifts. In truth, spiritual gifts are not about you. These gifts are all given to make Christ known. They are given at specific times for God's glory. Paul, the author of 1 Corinthians, strengthens this point by specifically discussing the unity of believers.

Read 1 Corinthians 12:12–27.

In the previous chapter, I discussed the idea of 120 individual tongues of fire resting above each Christian at Pentecost. Imagine how that would look now. How many tongues of fire would exist on Earth today if a fire burned above the head of every Christian? If you were able to orbit the globe and see the fires from outer space, how encouraging would that be? We are not alone and we are not meant to be alone. We are a royal priesthood. Every Christian serves God's kingdom with spiritual gifts. We are a God-empowered, global community, bound together by faith in Jesus Christ.

In 1 Corinthians 1, Paul uses the image of a body. His idea is terrific for seeing the value of living together for Christ. Trying to live for Jesus on our own would be like trying to live a life without thumbs. Try to do a few things without either of your thumbs and you'll be quickly frustrated. They are such a small percentage of your overall mass, yet so important to normal life. Some of us are thumbs. A few of us might be elbows. Wherever our particular function, each of us is a great addition to the body of Christ. We are a multitude of raging fires meant to reveal the greatness of Jesus Christ and His salvation to anyone who believes. *Together.*

———

If you are not a part of a faith community right now, you are missing out on some of the beauty that God designed for your life as a Christian. You aren't meant to be alone. You are meant to work together with other believers as a fully-functional body. A church helps you use your gifts and brings accountability to your life. You read God's Word with others and attempt to live for Him. It is a place where you know and are known by other people. It is hard to hide sin and selfishness in a true faith community.

Christians are called to follow God's teachings and seek out good works *because* of God's salvation. *Because* you are saved, you must live for Jesus. A lot of times, we get this backwards. We think that doing good things for God will earn us favor . . . or even salvation. We also think that if we do good, then somehow, God will owe us.

The Bible shows us is that God saves us through faith alone. Our salvation has nothing to do with being good. Our sole reason for doing good, for sharing God's love, for using our spiritual gifts, is *because* we have been saved and made right by Jesus Christ. Because of Christ, we are compelled to share with others what He has done. We live out the Great Commission in the world. We must tell people next door, in our cities, and around the world the Good News about Jesus Christ. We must do this *because* Jesus has saved, transformed, and made us right in the God's eyes.

It is great to know that you and I aren't meant to do this alone. We are called to do this together. Together, we let the world know of God's plan for salvation until Jesus returns.

While a long time has passed since Jesus ascended into heaven, you and I must not lose our urgency to tell others about Christ. As we are about to learn in the last chapter of this book, Jesus will return one day and judge the world. Those who believe in Jesus as Lord will be saved and spend eternity in heaven with God. Those who do not trust Jesus will experience eternal separation from God in hell. For this reason, we must faithfully live for Christ. We must tell others about Jesus.

We should not lose sight of what God has called us to do. The book of Hebrews tells us to stay focused. Hebrews 2:1 says, "Therefore we must pay much closer attention to what we have heard, lest we drift away from it." The image of drifting away is perfect. Imagine laying on an inflatable in a lake. You close your eyes, enjoying the moment. A few minutes later, you look up and realize you have floated far away from the shore. If you wait too long to look up, you'll drift too far!

The end is near. Christ will return; it may be during our lifetimes, maybe not. Either way, our job is to love God and live for Him. Our job is to tell the world about Jesus Christ until He returns. We must pay close attention. We must look up and stay focused on what God is calling us to do.

The author of Hebrews tells us to "consider how to stir up one another to love and good works, not neglecting to meet together, as is the habit of some, but encouraging one another, and all the more as you see the Day drawing near" (10:24, 25). I want you to think about this verse. This is a beautiful explanation of the Church. We stay close together and encourage one another. We lift each other up in faithfulness and accountability.

The community of believers is a priority because it reminds us of what Christ has done. We need each other to encourage our faithfulness and obedience to God. We can also help each other remember the truth that Jesus <u>will</u> come back . . . and that day is coming soon. Together, we are designed as Holy Spirit-empowered tongues of fire for God's glory, until He returns. Until The End.

Reflection

Read all of 1 Corinthians, chapter 12 again. Take your time. Think about what's been connected so far in God's story of redemption. Slow down; pretend this is the first time you've read this. Think about the words you are reading.

1. Jesus is coming back. When you consider the Great Commission, how does the urgency of Christ's return affect the way you feel about this calling?
2. Name a few ways you feel unprepared for sharing the Good News of Jesus with others.
3. 1 Corinthians 12:4–11 discusses spiritual gifts. Think of the ways your life changed when Christ saved you. How has God empowered you to accomplish the Great Commission?
4. If you think of the illustration of the church as one body, in what ways can you contribute to the local church for God's glory?
5. How has a church influenced your life? Think about a few ways God has used His church for your good.
6. What are some specific ways you can encourage other Christians and help them remain faithful to God's calling?

CHAPTER 12
The End

This is the end. When you look back at the stories you have read, do you see purpose? When you think about all that you've read, do you see God's design?

My first job in ministry was working with high school students. I landed an internship at a great church close to my college. I jumped at the chance to work with students. I loved every second of it. At the end of my first year, my boss called me into his office. "Jay, what do you think about working with Junior High students?" I didn't hesitate. "Middle schoolers? I'd hate that. They smell bad, they don't listen, and they aren't spiritually mature." My boss didn't hesitate either: "Well, if you want to keep your job . . ." With that one conversation I was in charge of the 6th, 7th, and 8th graders. That next year, I was stretched, to say the least.

After college, I headed off to seminary in a different city. One day, I received a phone call from a church. The first question they asked was, "Do you have experience working with junior high students?" Thanks to my old boss, I did. For the next seven years, I worked with 7th and 8th graders at that church. It was one of the finest ministry experiences in my life.

At the end of my time there, I felt a stirring to do something different. Through a series of conversations and interviews, I found myself the lead pastor of a small church. I was 29 years old and had a great many insecurities. I wasn't sure I was ready. I didn't know if I could lead adults as well as I had led students. I felt inexperienced and inadequate.

That little church started about six years before God called me as its pastor. It began with a core group of families with young children. Six years later, my first Sunday, I found myself ministering to families whose children were in junior high. At age 20, I was upset about having to work with junior high students. At age 29, I marveled at God's plan for my life. Sometimes you can't see God's plan until you look back at your past.

What is your story? When you think about your life, do you see God's design? While everything may not have been perfect, it is possible to see God's provision, protection, and comfort in your life. When you look back, I'm sure you will see God's design for your life.

God created the world. It was "very good" (Genesis 1:31). The Lord created Adam and Eve in perfect relationship with God. They walked and talked with God and enjoyed the beauty of all that He had created. God only gave one warning. He said, "but of the tree of the knowledge of good and evil you shall not eat, for in the day that you eat of it you shall surely die" (Genesis 2:17).

Adam and Eve believed the tree would bring them knowledge that would make them like God. They wanted something better than what they had. They disobeyed God and brought suffering, pain, and death to this world. It became broken—not as it was intended. Shortly after the beginning, everything was ruined.

But as we learned in chapter one of this book, God's first response to Adam and Eve's sin wasn't punishment. He offered redemption and hope. God spoke to the serpent and said, "I will put enmity between you and the woman, and between your offspring and her offspring; he shall bruise your head, and you shall bruise his heel" (Genesis 3:15).

This was the first time anyone heard about God's plan for redemption. The offspring of Eve would crush the head of the serpent. This was an allusion to Jesus' defeat of sin through His sacrifice. With His death, He paid sin's penalty for all of mankind. A perfect man died an undeserved death; His blood covered the sins of the world. Death was defeated when God raised Jesus back to life. The offspring of Eve may have been bruised, but the Son of God defeated sin and death.

Throughout this book, we have discovered the fullness of God's plan as it played out from Adam, to Jesus, to us. Now it's time to think about The End. While sin and death have been defeated, the effects of sin still remain in this world. But Jesus is coming back!

The disciple John was particularly close with Jesus. John, James, and Peter witnessed more miraculous moments than the rest of the apostles. John even referred to himself as "One of His disciples, whom Jesus loved" (John 13:23). John is also credited as the author of the Gospel of John, which gives the most explanation about Jesus' motives.

Most everyone in the early Church suffered for their faith. John was exiled to the island of Patmos because of his allegiance to Christ and for teaching God's Word (Revelation 1:9). While he was there, John had a vision of The End. God revealed it to him for our encouragement.

In the best way he knew how, John used man-made words to reveal the things God had shown him. There are many things in the Book of Revelation that are hard to understand. A few things however, are crystal clear. John reminds us of God's supreme authority and the importance of our faith in Christ. In Revelation 20, John tells of the Day of Judgement:

> *"Then I saw a great white throne and him who was seated on it. From his presence earth and sky fled away, and no place was found for them. And I saw the dead, great and small, standing before the throne, and books were opened. Then another book was opened, which is the book of life. And the dead were judged by what was written in the books, according to what they had done. And the sea gave up the dead who were in it, Death and Hades gave up the dead who were in them, and they were judged, each one of them, according to what they had done. Then Death and Hades were thrown into the lake of fire. This is the second death, the lake of fire. And if anyone's name was not found written in the book of life, he was thrown into the lake of fire" (Revelation 20:11–15).*

In this vision, Jesus has returned and is seated on a throne of judgment. The wording in verse eleven is fascinating to me. It sounds as if the earth and the sky can't be in the presence of God's holiness. They flee from the glory of God. In the presence of God, the books of life and judgement are read. Everyone is judged based on what they have done.

There will be two groups who will stand before God on that day: those who have rejected Christ and those who have believed. If you have faith in Jesus Christ, you are saved. God no longer sees your sin, but He sees what Jesus has done.

The Apostle Paul reminded the Galatians of this same idea, pointing out God's promise to Abraham.

> *"For in Christ Jesus you are all sons of God, through faith. For as many of you as were baptized into Christ have put on Christ. There is neither Jew nor*

Greek, there is neither slave nor free, there is no male and female, for you are all one in Christ Jesus. And if you are Christ's, then you are Abraham's offspring, heirs according to promise" (Galatians 3:26–29).

Followers of Jesus will be saved from death and destruction. We will be made new and a part of God's family in heaven forever. The book of life records our faith in Jesus. However, those who have rejected Jesus will experience punishment. Complete and total rejection of Jesus Christ will result in being thrown into the lake of fire. Rejection of Jesus is the only unforgiveable sin.

I don't believe the book of Revelation was written to create panic in the hearts of men. I believe it was written to show the utter consistency of God. What He promises, He will do. We have not only seen this in the big picture of God's design, but we have experienced it in our own lives. God has revealed His holiness to us. We know He is supremely in charge of all things. John's vision is a clear picture of how God will finally make everything right. He has brought salvation to all people through Jesus Christ. He defeated sin and death. His final step will be to recreate the earth. It will no longer be fallen and broken. God will make all things new.

"Then I saw a new heaven and a new earth, for the first heaven and the first earth had passed away, and the sea was no more. And I saw the holy city, new Jerusalem, coming down out of heaven from God, prepared as a bride adorned for her husband. And I heard a loud voice from the throne saying, 'Behold, the dwelling place of God is with man. He will dwell with them, and they will be his people, and God himself will be with them as their God'"
(Revelation 21:1–3).

There will be a new sky, a new earth, and no more sea. This is just a guess, but an earth with no sea seems like the reverse of Noah's flood. God has promised to never destroy the earth with another flood (Genesis 9:11). In this second creation, the sea has disappeared and everything is fresh.

107

A new city will drop from the sky, fully prepared for living. In his vision, John is reminded of a most special day. A bride spends countless hours making sure her ceremony is perfect. In the same way, God showed John a city so beautiful and full of promise that it reminded him of a wedding. God will redeem this fallen earth.

A new earth and a new city are pretty cool. But the thing that I truly cannot fathom is spending an eternity with God, unhindered by sin. Right now, believers in Jesus have the presence of the Holy Spirit in their lives. God is always with Christians. However, we still struggle with sin. We battle selfish desires every moment we are alive. (I have found myself praying to God, only to have my mind wander off to sinful places. I have been in glorious moments of worship, only to have anger overtake me.) Right now, we have only glimpses of perfection. Today, we are only able to experience God as much as our personal holiness allows. Because of sin, our relationships with God cannot be everything they will be in heaven. Think about what it means for God to dwell with man forever. This means you and I will be with God *for eternity*.

"He will wipe away every tear from their eyes, and death shall be no more, neither shall there be mourning, nor crying, nor pain anymore, for the former things have passed away.' And he who was seated on the throne said, 'Behold, I am making all things new.' Also he said, 'Write this down, for these words are trustworthy and true' (Revelation 21:4, 5).

No more death. What would it be like to never cry again? I can't comprehend what it would be like to wake up without aches and pain. Paul wrote, "Therefore, if anyone is in Christ, he is a new creation. The old has passed away; behold, the new has come" (2 Corinthians 5:17). We are a new creation in Christ, but the fullness of this understanding won't happen until we are free from sin. In The End, God will literally make everything new. All things will be made right. There will be no more suffering, shame, or sin.

The last thing God told John to do is to get his pen. God told him to "write this down, for these words are trustworthy and true"

(Revelation 21:5). When I read this, I consider all the things God has done throughout Scripture and also in my life. When I look back, I see purpose. I see God's design at work. Because of all God has done, I should completely trust what He will do. God has never failed. He has never broken a promise. God's faithfulness is perfect. Because of this, I can trust what will happen in The End.

God created. Man ruined. God promised salvation for the world and fulfilled that promise through Jesus Christ. Faith in Christ alone saves us. In Christ, we are given the Holy Spirit. With God's power in our lives, we are called to help the world see what God has done through Jesus.

We are called to share this Good News with everyone we know. This salvation isn't just for some people, it is for everyone. God has called and empowered us to be His messengers. We do this together, as the Church, until Christ returns. When He does, God will make all things right. The old will be gone; the new will come.

Those who reject Christ will experience full separation from God. Those who claim Christ will spend an eternity in heaven with God. It's going to happen in The End. It's God's plan and His design.

The last thing John wrote in Revelation is a great reminder. Jesus says, "Surely I am coming soon" (Revelation 22:20). Jesus *is* coming back. We can trust this promise because of all the things we've seen from Scripture. We can trust this promise because God has always been absolutely consistent.

When I look back, I see God's design in all things. It gives me confidence in what He will do. The design of God's Word helps me to trust Him. God is faithful, good, and true.

You have seen His plan. You now know the design. My prayer is that you will trust God with your past, your today, and whatever the future brings. You can trust God with your life because you've seen His design.

Reflection

Read Revelation 20:11–15 and Revelation 21:1–5 again. Take your time. Think about what's been connected so far in God's story of redemption. Slow down; pretend this is the first time you've read this. Think about the words you are reading.

1. What is your story? When you think about your life, in what ways do you see God's plan?
2. How does God's faithfulness throughout the Bible bring you encouragement?
3. When you read Revelation 20:11–15, how does it make you feel? In what ways does the Good News of Jesus Christ encourage you?
4. What do you imagine God's new heaven and earth to be like? As you think about this, how do you picture eternity?
5. What specific things in your life do you look forward to God redeeming and making new?
6. How does knowing that Jesus will return change the way you live today?

What Now?

Hopefully, by reading this book, you have seen a clearer picture of God's design throughout Scripture. As you turn this final page, don't consider this the end, but the beginning. I hope you will open your Bible with confidence in the days to come. I hope you feel empowered to dig deeper and grow in your faith. God's Word will help you live for Jesus.

The Bible will help you understand God better. Scripture can show you what you are called to do as a Christian. Not a word is wasted. All of God's Word tells of His design. I hope you will love and follow God's Word.

Know this: if you claim Christ, you have been equipped to do good things for His glory. Just as Paul tells Timothy, knowing Scripture will change your life.

"All Scripture is breathed out by God and profitable for teaching, for reproof, for correction, and for training in righteousness, that the man of God may be complete, equipped for every good work" (2 Timothy 3:16–17).

Take your newfound understanding of God and His Word and keep going! Let your life shine brightly for God's glory. Until Jesus comes back, let us all grow in faithfulness to Him. Until His return, point people to Jesus.

Grace and peace.

Notes

1. Philip Graham Ryken and R. Kent Hughes, *Exodus: Saved for God's Glory* (Wheaton, IL: Crossway Books, 2005), 216.

2. www.youtube.com/embed/HkEX0eb2eBo?start=0&end=177

3. John N. Oswalt, *The Book of Isaiah Chapters 1-39*, *New International Commentary on the Old Testament* (Grand Rapids, MI: Eerdmans Publishing Co.), 4.

4. John B. Polhill, The New American Commentary: *Acts* (Nashville, TN: Broadman Press, 1992), 97-98.

Made in the USA
Columbia, SC
27 February 2018